GOD THE STRANGER

Reflections About Resurrection

EDMUND A. STEIMLE

FORTRESS PRESS   PHILADELPHIA

The chapters in this book were first presented as radio sermons on the NBC network's National Radio Pulpit series, April 2–June 25, 1978, under the auspices of the Broadcasting and Film Commission of the National Council of the Churches of Christ in the United States of America.

Library of Congress Cataloging in Publication Data

Steimle, Edmund A
God the stranger.

"First presented as radio sermons on the NBC network's National radio pulpit series, April 2-June 25, 1978."
Includes bibliographical references.
1. Easter—Sermons. 2. Sermons, American.
3. Lutheran Church—Sermons. I. National radio pulpit.
II. Title.
BV4259.S73   252'.63   78-14674
ISBN 0-8006-1354-6

7410J78   Printed in the United States of America   1-1354

Contents

Easter — Festival of Mystery

And when the sabbath was past, Mary Magdalene, and Mary the mother of James, and Salome, bought spices, so that they might go and anoint him. And very early on the first day of the week they went to the tomb when the sun had risen. And they were saying to one another, "Who will roll away the stone for us from the door of the tomb?" And looking up, they saw that the stone was rolled back; for it was very large. And entering the tomb, they saw a young man sitting on the right side, dressed in a white robe; and they were amazed. And he said to them, "Do not be amazed; you seek Jesus of Nazareth, who was crucified. He has risen, he is not here; see the place where they laid him. But go, tell his disciples and Peter that he is going before you to Galillee; there you will see him, as he told you." And they went out and fled from the tomb; for trembling and astonishment had come upon them; and they said nothing to any one, for they were afraid.

—Mark 16:1–8

A couple of weeks ago several of us were talking about Easter and someone asked, "I wonder why everyone makes such a big deal out of Christmas, while Easter comes and goes and it doesn't cut much ice, really."

And it's true of course. The Christmas celebration goes on for weeks: stores and streets and homes festooned with holly and ribbons and lights in the windows, trees and greens all over the place, carols by the score, bells ringing on street corners, gifts, parties, the creche, the family reunions. The whole world is turned on its ear at Christmas—and for weeks at a time.

But Easter—except for a few of the faithful who have gone through Ash Wednesday on down to Good Friday—it's pretty much a one-day affair. The world—except for a flurry of lilies, an Easter parade on Fifth Avenue, Easter eggs and bunnies for the children, the annual invasion of Fort Lauderdale, a few new clothes (fewer now than in the past), and an occasional sing-along of Handel's *Messiah*—the world takes little notice. No lights in the windows or bells on the streets, and how come there are so very few Easter carols?

It's strange, really. For if there were no Easter, there'd be no Christmas. If the child had grown up and died . . . period, who today would remember the magic night of his birth? For no Resurrection story, then no New Testament, no church, no Christianity. Easter was of course the first Christian holiday, and the Christmas holiday didn't come along until much, much later. So why does Easter cut so little ice in the world today, compared with Christmas?

Maybe it's the difference between dawn or dusk and high noon. We're grateful for the sun at high noon of course, but it doesn't do much to us in evoking imagination or yearning or poetry. There's no mystery to it. Even the birds sing at dusk and dawn, but at high noon, when the sun is at its zenith, they are quiet.

Maybe we've been looking at Easter in the wrong way, so as to miss its mystery and its intrigue.

Frederick Buechner tells of the night he stood on the bridge of a small British freighter somewhere near the middle of the Atlantic:

> I was talking to a young officer with red hair who told me something that is very useful to know. He had been looking around to see if he could spot the lights of any other ships on the horizon, and what he told me was this: the way to see lights on the horizon is not to look at the horizon, but to look at the sky just above it. And I discovered that he was right. This is the way to do it. Since then I have learned that it is also the way to see other things.
>
> I do not think that I would have looked straight at the tomb if I had been there (on that first day of the week so long ago), at the large boulder that they had rolled up to seal it with. I do not think that I would have even if I had wanted to, in that queer, seething light between night and daybreak when you cannot look long at anything before it begins to disappear. I would have looked just above it, or off to one side.

Maybe if we would do that on Easter, look at the Resurrection out of the corner of the eye as it were, we'd see more of the mystery and intrigue in the story of Easter—and perhaps end up wanting to sing more carols! For once you take your eyes off the glare of the sun, the bare unvarnished fact of it—that Christ is risen, you become aware of the rough edges, the unfinished stories, the question marks which surround it. One New Testament scholar notes that it is significant that both death and Resurrection take place in darkness: "events too sacred to be gazed on, too full of portent to be plainly seen."

Robert Neale suggests that there are three responses to the sacred dimensions of life: the magical, the profane, and the religious. With respect to Easter, the profane response is obvious, and both misses the fact of it and also defuses its mystery: to call it no more for example than an hallucination or the lingering memory of Jesus among his followers, as Lincoln for example is "alive" in the memory of those who revere him; or to speak of the immortality of the soul of Jesus, which—if true—certainly cannot account for either the surprise or consternation or joy of the witnesses to his Resurrection. The profane response denies both the mystery and the miracle.

The magical response is simply to take it all too literally: the flat and unadorned resuscitation of a corpse, a "bodily resurrection" in the sense which Paul explodes in that mysterious account where he says that "the perishable does not inherit the imperishable," that the body is raised a "spiritual body"—whatever that means— as he says, "Lo! I tell you a mystery."

The religious response, on the other hand, would be to look at the Resurrection out of the corner of the eye rather than directly, to catch the mystery and the wonder of it.

Once you do that you notice, out of the corner of the eye, that the initial reaction to Christ alive is not a huge sigh of relief, or unfettered joy, or a covey of hallelujahs as you might expect, but embarrassment, fear, almost terror. So the New English Bible, in its translation of the Easter narratives, uses words like terrified, dumfounded, beside themselves with terror, falling prostrate before him. Even the New Testament scholar Günther Bornkamm, who comes right out and says that the story of the women at the tomb in Mark is "obviously a legend," nevertheless exclaims, "[But see] how his story is told! The wonderful event of the Resurrection is not even depicted, such is the reticence and awe."

Why then "the reticence and awe," the embarrassment and the fear? Well, for one thing, it means that we cannot escape the startling ways in which God acts. Obviously the women, the disciples, the followers of Jesus were disillusioned and in despair in the face of his death—all their hopes and dreams smashed, quite literally. So they wept at the cross and on the way to the tomb. But they quickly came to accept it. They went with their spices to anoint him—precisely to outsmell the smell of death. That little detail underlines how quickly they learned to accept the death and live with it. For does not all life end so? You and I quickly learn to come to terms with grief and disillusionment and death. We learn to live with it. We have to.

So part of their embarrassment and fear at the thought of Christ alive was the sudden realization that God would act *through* suffering and disillusionment and death. To be sure, they'd had their hopes, their dreams, all the promises of abundant life he'd held out to them. But never in their wildest moments had they considered that God would accomplish his vast purpose of love and liberation *through* death and suffering and disillusionment. It's one thing to come to terms with death, to live with it and accept it. We all have to do that. It's quite another to be faced with the hard reality that this is how God acts, how he works out his purpose for the world—for you, for me. But now they knew. God does not save us *from* suffering and death. He saves us *through* it. "Take up your cross and follow me" was no longer one possibility, one option among others, to be held at arm's length alongside some other possible options conceivably less stringent. Now it was there, smack in front of them. Life—abundant life—is not cheap. So they were embarrassed, amazed, terror-stricken.

And that leads directly to this: before Easter brings its inevitable joy, it brings judgment. And no doubt that's what terrified them too. For as they buried him in the tomb, they buried not only their hopes and dreams and all the promises he had held out to them, all the love and care and compassion he had shown—all this was buried with him. But that was not all. They also buried with him their uncertain faith, their shabby quarrels as to who was to be greatest in the kingdom, their petty jealousies and impatience with him, the ugly scenes of denial and betrayal—all this was buried with him too. And in that burial, as Tillich has reminded us, is the powerful symbol of being forgotten. As they buried him, they also buried the fact that they all forsook him and fled when the chips were down, in the not unreasonable hope that the unpleasantness would soon be forgotten too.

No wonder they were amazed and afraid on that first Resurrection morning. For all this was now alive again: the promises, the love, the vibrant life they had known, to be sure, but all the sad betrayals and pettiness and sleeping while he was agonizing in the garden too. It had all come back. Death was no longer a forgetting; it was a remembering.

So the most characteristic initial word on Easter is not "Be of good cheer," but "Be not afraid." For the one who is risen, who brings it all back to life again, is the one we know. And with recognition, the fear, the embarrassment, turn into joy: "Then were the disciples glad when they saw the Lord." So Easter becomes a commentary on John's words: "There is no fear in love, for perfect love casts out fear." One of the mysteries of Easter is precisely that we can rejoice and sing our hallelujahs—at the moment that we are shown up for what we really are and have been.

And then there's one more mystery when you look at the Resurrection out of the corner of the eye: the strange fact that Christ was seen alive only by those who had been his friends, his disciples, his followers. No appearance to Pilate or Herod, or to the Sanhedrin or the scribes and Pharisees—to those who had opposed him and engineered his death. I wonder why. Think of the bewildering impact of a miraculous appearance at Herod's court, at a royal banquet between the soup course and the entrée! And beyond that, even to his closest followers he is apparently not immediately recognizable. Mistaken for a gardener, or a stranger walking along the road with them. Why this strange reticence? Is God shy, perhaps?

Yes, in a sense I suppose he is. For if you have ever known what it is to be loved at all, how did it come to you? There must be some openness to it, some resonance. For it beckons. It intrigues. It invites. And when you respond to it, then bells ring, birds sing, and your whole world is flooded with joy and light. And your immediate impulse is to throw flowers around and sing hallelujahs. He is risen. He is not here.

Today in our celebration of Easter there is a great gulf fixed between Good Friday and Easter. For those who do pay any attention to Good Friday any longer, it is pretty much a day of unrelieved gloom and sadness and despair, a day of death. While Easter, in our day, is pretty much a day of unrelieved joy and singing and flowers, for all is well. There are reasons for this, maybe some good reasons. But it may well result in obscuring or even wiping out the mystery that is God. For in olden times these two days were celebrated together: cross and crown, death and life, defeat and victory. For the mystery of God is revealed both in pain and death *and* in Resurrection and life. For where there is mystery there is great pain, but where there is mystery there is also great laughter.

And for those who in pain or bewilderment or loneliness or fear lift up their tentative hands and faces in hope to see his face, this shy God of love responds with great laughter: He is risen; he is not here.

The Stranger

That very day two of them were going to a village named Emmaus,
about seven miles from Jerusalem, and talking with each other about all
these things that had happened. While they were talking and discussing
together, Jesus himself drew near and went with them. But their eyes
were kept from recognizing him. And he said to them, "What is this
conversation which you are holding with each other as you walk?" And
they stood still, looking sad. Then one of them, named Cleopas,
answered him, "Are you the only visitor to Jerusalem who does not
know the things that have happened there in these days?" And he said
to them, "What things?" And they said to him, "Concerning Jesus of
Nazareth, who was a prophet mighty in deed and word before God and
all the people, and how our chief priests and rulers delivered him up
to be condemned to death, and crucified him. But we had hoped that
he was the one to redeem Israel. Yes, and besides all this, it is now the
third day since this happened. Moreover, some women of our company
amazed us. They were at the tomb early in the morning and did not find
his body; and they came back saying that they had even seen a vision of
angels, who said that he was alive. Some of those who were with us
went to the tomb, and found it just as the women had said; but him
they did not see." And he said to them, "O foolish men, and slow of
heart to believe all that the prophets have spoken! Was it not necessary
that the Christ should suffer these things and enter into his glory?" And
beginning with Moses and al the prophets, he interpreted to them in all
the scriptures the things concerning himself.

So they drew near to the village to which they were going. He
appeared to be going further, but they constrained him, saying, "Stay
with us, for it is toward evening and the day is now far spent." So he
went in to stay with them. When he was at table with them, he took the
bread and blessed, and broke it, and gave it to them. And their eyes
were opened and they recognized him; and he vanished out of their
sight. Then they said to each other, "Did not our hearts burn within
us while he talked to us on the road, while he opened to us the
scriptures?" And they rose that same hour and returned to Jerusalem;
and they found the eleven gathered together and those who were with

them, who said, "The Lord has risen indeed, and has appeared to
Simon!" Then they told what had happened on the road, and how he
was known to them in the breaking of the bread.   —Luke 24:13–35

The story of the walk to Emmaus is one of the loveliest stories in
the New Testament, certainly the most intriguing of the appearance
stories following the Resurrection. But it has positively sinister
implications for you and me some two thousand years later. If the
risen Christ walking and talking with two of his disciples is un-
recognizable, how are you and I ever to recognize God's presence
with us today? If the risen Christ is a stranger to his own disciples,
how much more of a stranger will God seem to us twenty centuries
later?

That part of the story, that he was not recognized, is baffling.
Presumably they had been in daily contact with him for the better
part of three years. And now they do not even recognize him. What
goes on here? Was he wearing a disguise? But what of his voice?
His familiar clothing? His mannerisms, the way he walked? All
those familiar characteristics of a close friend that lead us to recognition even after years of separation—but they had been separated
for only three days. "But their eyes were kept from recognizing
him." Why was this so?

Well, for one thing, we have to remember that it was the *crucified* Jesus who was raised from the dead and appeared to the
disciples. And it was the crucified Jesus who they were unprepared
to recognize as the Christ, even before the death. Remember, "they
all forsook him and fled." And if they were unprepared to recognize him for what he was in death, they were equally unprepared
to recognize the crucified Christ in the appearances after the Resurrection. After all, if he was the Christ, God would not let him die,
would he? And die in disgrace at the hands of the religious establishment in Jerusalem? It was all too much.

And after it was all over and they were making their lonely way
to Emmaus, even if the tales of the women having seen him alive
were true, he wouldn't appear as a stranger along the road with
them, would he? Where was the blinding Resurrection light? The
angels? The hallelujah chorus? It was all far too ordinary, too
undramatic, calmly interpreting Scripture to them as if nothing had
happened, like some hotshot Christian whipping out his pocket

New Testament to tell us what the good old Book really has to say. So "their eyes were kept from recognizing him." Their eyes were kept because of their preconceived notions of how God would and would not act. They were blinded by their expectations of how God would and would not act.

But this was nothing new, really. This had been so before the events of the past three days. Jesus was different. He met no one's expectations. As Hans Küng writes:

> He did not belong to the establishment nor to the revolutionary party, but neither did he want to opt out of ordinary life, to be an ascetic monk. Obviously he did not adopt the role which a saint or a seeker after holiness, or even a prophet, is frequently expected to play. For this he was too normal in his clothing, his eating habits, his general behavior. . . . [So he became a] *skandalon,* a small stone over which one might stumble. . . . He was attacked on all sides. He had not played any of the expected roles: for those who supported law and order he turned out to be a provocateur, dangerous to the system. He disappointed the activist revolutionaries by his nonviolent love of peace. . . . he offended the passive, world-forsaking ascetics by his uninhibited worldliness. And for the devout who adapted themselves to the world he was too uncompromising. For the silent majority he was too noisy and for the noisy minority he was too quiet, too gentle for the strict and too strict for the gentle. He was an obvious outsider.

He was different—a stranger.

And if all this was true then, why should it be any different now? If Christ is really the clue to who and what God is and how God acts, God will not fit into *our* notions of how God should and should not act either. Most of us tend to domesticate God, that is, make God fit into our notions of how God should act. So God becomes the patron saint of a democratic, capitalist system. God blesses America and hates the communists even more than we do. God becomes a gargantuan, blown-up version of *me* in my better moments. God should be comfortable and folksy; close, not far; forgiving, not judging; giving us comfort and peace of mind rather than asking us to deny ourselves and follow him.

A couple of years ago I was giving a series of sermons during a week at a summer assembly. At the end of the week an elderly gentleman came up and after some complimentary remarks about my preaching went on to say that he didn't agree at all with one of the sermons, in which I had attempted to point out that God in his nearness can be known only in contrast with God in his distance, based on Isaiah's startling vision of God in the temple filled with smoke and the song of the seraphim: "Holy, holy, holy is the Lord of hosts." He said to me, "God is not far . . . I've got him in my heart." Very cozy. There is a sense of course in which God *can* be known in our hearts, but the God of the Bible, the God revealed in the living Christ, also stands over against us in our "hearts." We do not take him captive in our hearts. Indeed *he* may take *us* captive in our hearts, and then perhaps we can know the peace of God which passes all understanding. But it is precisely beyond our understanding because God, if Christ is the clue to his nature, is different. He is surprising, like appearing as a stranger along the dusty road to Emmaus.

Now there is a strange sort of comfort in all this. Perhaps when we are baffled by the way God apparently works in our world, he may be closer to us than we realize—as the disciples discovered when they arrived at Emmaus: "Did not our hearts burn within us while he talked to us along the road?" So even in our experience of the absence of God there may be the experience of his presence —as Tillich points out—"in the empty space that cries out to be filled by him." So when prayer goes unanswered, or we are overwhelmed with tragedy—with cancer or a crippling stroke or the family falling apart—or there is senseless terrorism and grinding poverty and blatant racism, the fact that our experience or lack of experience of God points to a mystery, the mystery of *no* experience of God in the way in which we expect, precisely *there* may be the possibility of meeting the stranger along the road.

But before the story ended, the stranger did become recognizable in the breaking of bread. They had invited him in to stay with them. And "when he was at table with them, he took the bread and blessed and broke it and gave it to them. And their eyes were opened and they recognized him."

For the early church there is little question that this pointed to the experience of the living Christ in the Sacrament, the Eucharist. And that may also be true for us. As the community of believers gathers about the table set with bread and wine, and we hear the ancient words, "Take, eat; this is my body . . . take, drink; this is the blood of the New Testament," and are reminded both of the death and at the same time of the hope of a great banquet in the future, our eyes may then be opened too, so that we recognize the stranger for what he really is.

But such recognition may not be limited solely to the cultic act of the Sacrament. No doubt it was the familiar words or gestures that did it. The familiar words of the blessing may come to us today in reassurance and hope on the lips of a familiar friend, or a member of the family, or even a preacher. Or the familiar words of the blessing may come to us in the expression of care and concern by someone familiar to us, and we are comforted and encouraged and given hope. Reminded of days and hours when God was familiar rather than strange, we are encouraged and given hope that Christ is indeed alive and that God, for all his strangeness, is faithful to his promises to be with us always, even to the end of the age.

Or contrariwise, the stranger may be recognizable when you and I respond in love and concern and thoughtfulness to the needs of another. As John says in the Fourth Gospel, "He that wills to *do* shall know." I can remember in my last parish that when I was down in the dumps, discouraged, uncertain of the reality of God, I would go to the hospital and visit with patients from my parish, offering what I could of reassurance and comfort and hope in God's presence and care, and then the God who may have been a stranger to me earlier became recognizable in the breaking of bread.

But it may be that he becomes recognizable on the lips of unlikely people. It was many years ago, shortly after the end of World War II, and I was in the shop of a friendly neighborhood tailor whose name was Mr. Birnbaum. And he stopped me as I was leaving and said in his thick accent, "Mr. Steimle, I have a problem. As you know, I am a Jew and my wife, she is a Christian. Her brother was a violent Nazi when we were in Germany. He hated me and did nothing to help us. He was happy to get rid of us when we came over here. But now he is in a prison camp and he has written us asking us to send him some food. My wife, she says No, we send him nothing. But I say Yes, we should send him something. What do you think, Mr. Steimle?" I don't know how you would have felt, but I felt humble and ashamed. Ashamed of his Christian wife possibly, but even more ashamed of myself for being unprepared to find the stranger God recognizable on the lips of a pleasant Jewish neighborhood tailor.

And then the story ends abruptly: "And he vanished out of their sight." Which is to say, you can't nail God down to a dining room table and the breaking of bread any more than you can nail God down to a cross with real nails, for that matter. They wanted him to stay. They wanted to rehash this marvelous experience. But God would have no part in deadly-boring postmortems, as at a bridge table; "he vanished out of their sight."

"The stranger comes suddenly out of nowhere [as another puts it] like the first clear light of the sun after a thunderstorm, or maybe like the thunder itself, and· maybe we recognize him and maybe we don't." But maybe we can reach the point where we can bless God not merely for his recognizable presence, but precisely because he is different, unpredictable, breaking away from our stultifying expectations, precisely because he does come as the stranger into our lives to give assurance and pardon and hope.

The Perplexing Problem of
Suffering and God's Power

*Servants, be submissive to your masters with all respect, not only to the
kind and gentle but also to the overbearing. For one is approved if,
mindful of God, he endures pain while suffering unjustly. For what
credit is it, if when you do wrong and are beaten for it you take it
patiently? But if when you do right and suffer for it you take it patiently,
you have God's approval. For to this you have been called, because
Christ also suffered for you, leaving you an example, that you should
follow in his steps. He committed no sin; no guile was found on his
lips. When he was reviled, he did not revile in return; when he suffered,
he did not threaten; but he trusted to him who judges justly. He himself
bore our sins in his body on the tree, that we might die to sin and live
to righteousness. By his wounds you have been healed. For you were
straying like sheep, but have now returned to the Shepherd and
Guardian of your souls.* —1 Peter 2:18–25

Jubilate—"Make a joyful noise unto the Lord"—that was the
ancient name given to the third Sunday after Easter. Appropriate
enough, one would think, for the entire Easter season, where the
joy simply cannot be bottled up into one day.

But here's a strange circumstance: in each of the three lessons
traditionally appointed for Jubilate Sunday there is a strong under-
current of pain, suffering, injustice. The Old Testament lesson
(Isaiah 40:25–31) for example is taken from the time of the exile,
which someone has called the "age of the absence of God," and you
hear the exiles singing their sad songs by the rivers of Babylon:
"My way is hid from the Lord and my right is disregarded by my
God." Then in the Gospel lesson (John 16:16–23) there is the
unexpected announcement of death and separation, when Christ
says, "You will weep and lament, but the world will rejoice; you
will be sorrowful, but your sorrow will be turned into joy." But
it's a strange sort of joy out of sorrow which comes out in the New

Testament Epistle: "Beloved, I beseech you as aliens and exiles . . . for one is approved if, mindful of God, he endures pain while suffering unjustly." You would think, wouldn't you, that if he is mindful of God he would enter wholeheartedly into the Jubilate, into the Easter joy of victory over death and sufferings, instead of enduring pain while suffering unjustly.

So what goes on here? Well, what goes on is that the church year is far more realistic than we are. We tend to chop up the Christian year into moments of joy and moments of gloom, each unmixed and unadulterated. Rejoice for all you're worth on Christmas and Easter—all's well! And then give yourself to despondency and gloom in Lent and on Good Friday, for all's not well. But the church year, reflecting the stark realism of the Bible, is never so black or white. Christmas, "joy to the world," is followed on December 26th by Saint Stephen's Day, in remembrance of the first Christian martyr, and two days later by the Day of Holy Innocents, recalling the massacre of the children in Bethlehem and the surrounding countryside. "O little town of Bethlehem, how still . . .", how sweet—running with the blood of children in celebration of the child's birth!

So here in the middle of Easter rejoicing, these haunting lessons marked by exile and God's absence, by pain and suffering, are to remind us that death can come on Easter—as it did a few years ago in our family—just as birth occurs on Good Friday. Birth in death and death in life.

Now granted the realism of it all, true to life no doubt, doesn't the realism point to the unbearable problem which apparently is left unresolved by the Christian faith: How can you possibly believe in a good God in a world like this? After all, what sense does it really make if children are massacred because of the birth of a child, or if "enduring pain while suffering unjustly" a man is "approved by God"? What sort of God is this anyway? Dr. Carl Goerdeler, a devout Christian and a leader in the resistance movement in Nazi Germany, wrote in final despair a few days before he was executed by the Gestapo for his part in the plot on Hitler's life: "[God] lets millions of decent people suffer and die without raising a finger. Is this justice? . . . What a botcher of a God who knows the wrongdoers and the apostates and punishes the upright and the faithful. No, it is inconceivable . . . like the Psalmist . . .

I argue with God because I do not understand him. 'Whom he loves, he takes early to himself.' No, that is not comfort; it is intolerable." Albert Camus echoes the same despair in trying to understand the Christian God: "I share with you the same revulsion from evil. But I do not share your hope, and I continue to struggle against this universe in which children suffer and die."

Well, what shall we say? What can we say? Obviously there are no easy answers, indeed no answer at all that can "explain" it satisfactorily. Not that men haven't tried, as I have too on more than one occasion. But all the answers are forced to skirt around the edges of the problem and never really can get to the heart of it. Job's "comforters," you may recall, were of small comfort since they equated suffering with the punishment of sin, which didn't seem to fit Job's situation at all. And the answer, if you can call it that, that Job got in the end was the answer that there really is no answer: "I am God"—said God out of the whirlwind—"and who are you, Job?" When you get to the New Testament, Jesus puts the quietus on the old Jewish notion—which still nags at our insides sometimes—that suffering is somehow related to some dark sin in the past. Remember when the disciples asked him, "Rabbi, who sinned, this man or his parents, that he was born blind?" And Jesus replied, "It was not that this man sinned, this man or his parents, but that the works of God might be made manifest in him." And that merely clears up one problem to raise another. What dark saying is that, "that the works of God might be made manifest in him"—a man born blind!

The heart of the whole problem, it seems to me, is the problem of God's power. If God is almighty—which he must be if he is God—then how can we square his love with his power? How can God be all-powerful and all-loving at the same time in a world like ours? He can be one or the other perhaps, but how both? The popular slogan of a few years ago, God is dead, is really one way of answering the problem. Or the phrase "the absence of God," the sound of which echoes and reechoes throughout the pages of the Bible as well as in the secret chamber of our hearts, is another way of approaching the problem. "Why art thou so far from helping me?" is another way of saying, "Why, for heaven's sake, doesn't God use his power in the world and do something about the suffering, the senseless sorrow and pain, the tragic waste?"

Without holding out any false hopes of solving or explaining the problem, it may help us to understand the problem a little if we recall how the ancient Jews and the early Christians came to know anything about God at all in the first place. Because Genesis, with its account of the power of God creating the world, comes first in the Bible, we are apt to think that this is the normal sequence: power first, to which we then try to add or fit or inject the character of love. But in the experience of the Jews it was just the reverse. The earliest accounts of the Jews' experience of God begins with his care, his love: the deliverance of the people from slavery in Egypt; the covenant with the people at Sinai where he promises to be with them; the journey through the wilderness with God present with them despite their grumblings, rebellion, and despair. Only later—much later—did they think of this God in terms of the Creator, Ruler over galaxies of stars and the laws of the universe. What they knew of God in the first place was simply God *with* them. John Courtney Murray, the distinguished Jesuit scholar, points out that when Moses asked God his name, the reply came: "My name is 'I shall be there, with you, in power.' " Which still leaves us with the problem of power.

When you come to the New Testament, and this God makes himself known in Christ, he comes in weakness rather than in the kind of power we associate with the word *God.* He comes as a child, as a suffering servant, as a man who dies—and *then* as one raised from the dead. It's as if God were saying, "Do you really want to see divine power at work? Then discard your human notions of power and look at the way this Son of mine lives and dies." To be sure, the tempter is always at his elbow suggesting the use of power as you and I would like to see it operate: Turn stones into bread, cast yourself down from the temple, and if you really are the Son of God, come down from the cross. But as often as the tempter tugged at his sleeve, just so often came the reply: "Thou shalt not tempt the Lord thy God." In other words, thou shalt not tempt the Lord thy God to use his power the way the world—you and I—expect it to be used.

God's power is clothed in the weakness of love and suffering and pain. This takes a bit of getting used to, and we obviously haven't gotten used to it yet! A scandal to the Jews, foolishness to the Greeks, and sheer absurdity to most of us still.

But suppose we do turn it around—take the power in our hands, for example, and try to fill it with love and concern. Is the result any less absurd? We have made tremendous strides in medicine in recent years, in the power to prolong life and dull pain and suffering. No question about it, this is a tremendous humanitarian advance. But look at some of the absurd results: the proliferation of older people who live beyond what they feel are years of usefulness and potential joy, often merely a burden to somebody else, and then when the end approaches, often all too gradually, there is the slow deterioration of mind and body until sometimes just a breathing husk of life remains for weeks, even months sometimes. Often there is no pain, fortunately, but how long shall this husk, this life, if you can still call it that, be preserved? And so we sometimes ask the doctors not to take heroic measures to prolong the life, since what's the purpose? You won't misunderstand! This is in no way to deplore the tremendous advances medical science has been able to accomplish in prolonging life and in easing pain and suffering. It is only to raise the question whether power motivated by our understanding of love solves the problem. Other problems are created almost equally absurd and frustrating. We cannot easily escape the absurdity of life.

So we come back to the basic question. How do we know God at all? How do you know even if there is a God? Nature with all its grandeur and beauty and obvious and mysterious power gives an ambiguous answer of course: sunset and hurricane; the gorgeous unfolding of a bud in spring, and the terror of earthquake and flood; the flashing colors of a butterfly, and the flashing colors of a bird which chops up the flashing colors of the butterfly for food.

And the long stream of history gives an even more ambiguous answer: the truly great achievements in medical science, and Dachau; the powerful forces for justice and peace, and a napalm bomb burning a Vietnamese village to a crisp; the awesome power of nuclear fission, and what? Nagasaki, or a city glowing with light and humming with modern conveniences. Find God in the confused and surging tides of history down through the ages if you can. I can't. It's a mishmash. Or find God in the depths of your existence? Go off alone to find him in the deepest recesses in your heart? If your heart is anything like mine, it's a desperate tangle of darkness and light. At least for me, contemplation is no ultimate answer.

I have been able to discern an unmistakable clue to the nature of

God at only one point: in this strange and admittedly absurd story of Jesus of Nazareth, the man for others, the one man who is truly human, the man who is what I know in my tangled heart I should be and was meant to be, whom God raised from the dead as if to say, "Amen. Let it be so. Find me here in apparent weakness and you shall get a glimpse of what my power really means."

And though the problem remains, at least one thing comes clear. The power of God is not primarily a resource to get us out of pain and suffering and death. Every temptation our Lord had to meet was in one way or another a temptation to escape suffering and death. Yet we continue to think of God's power almost exclusively in those terms. Of course it's understandable, and particularly when we are concerned about the suffering others have to endure. But the strange answer from the New Testament is not "I will save you from these things," but "Lo, I am with you always, even unto the end of the age."

So Bonhoeffer writes: "God is teaching us that we must live as men who can get along very well without him. . . . God allows himself to be edged out of the world, and that is exactly the way, the only way, in which he can be with us to help us." What I understand him to be saying here is in effect that so long as we begin with God's power and try to use it in our behalf we inevitably try to become little gods ourselves. But if we begin with Christ and see Christ as God's promise to be with us no matter what, then we begin to know what faith—what trust in God's power—really means: no miracles to pop us out of our problems, any more than a miracle saved our Lord from the cross; but a Resurrection as God's Amen to Christ's way of serving others with the assurance that God's power is with us in whatever it may be that life throws up at us.

This is no simple answer to the problem of God all-powerful and all-loving and the perplexing presence of evil and suffering and death in the world. But it may give us a different perspective from which to view the problem and live through it. So to the exiles, after the prophet had pointed to the mighty power of God in nature and in history, he indicates the purpose of it all: "He gives power to the faint, and to him who has no might he increases strength. . . . they who wait for the Lord shall renew their strength, they shall mount up on wings like eagles, they shall run and not be weary, they shall walk and not faint." So too, Peter: "For one is approved if, mindful of God, he endures pain while suffering unjustly." For this is precisely how God showed his mighty power in a cross and Resurrection. We are never given an explanation, but an assurance of a presence, a power which enables us not to escape, but to live through the absurdity of a world of evil and pain and suffering, and the power to overcome it.

What It Means To Be a Christian

*"Let not your hearts be troubled; believe in God, believe also in me.
In my Father's house are many rooms; if it were not so, would I have
told you that I go to prepare a place for you? And when I go and
prepare a place for you, I will come again and will take you to myself,
that where I am you may be also. And you know the way where I am
going." Thomas said to him, "Lord, we do not know where you are
going; how can we know the way?" Jesus said to him, "I am the way,
and the truth, and the life; no one comes to the Father, but by me.
If you had known me, you would have known my Father also;
henceforth you know him and have seen him."*

*Philip said to him, "Lord, show us the Father, and we shall be
satisfied." Jesus said to him, "Have I been with you so long, and yet you
do not know me, Philip? He who has seen me has seen the Father; how
can you say, 'Show us the Father'? Do you not believe that I am in the
Father and the Father in me? The words that I say to you I do not speak
on my own authority; but the Father who dwells in me does his works.
Believe me that I am in the Father and the Father in me; or else
believe me for the sake of the works themselves.*

*"Truly, truly, I say to you, he who believes in me will do the works
that I do; and greater works than these will he do, because I go to the
Father."* —John 14:1–12

There are a lot of queer ideas going around on what it means to be
a Christian.

For example, there are some who say that it means to believe
certain propositions about Jesus, God, and the Bible, that is, to
believe that Jesus was the Son of God or that he was born of a
virgin, or that the Godhead involves three persons, or that the Bible
is the inerrant Word of God, or to believe in the bodily Resurrection of Jesus from the dead (and what they mean by *bodily* is
obscure since the biblical accounts of the Resurrection make it
abundantly clear that the Resurrection is far more than the mere
resuscitation of a corpse). Now all these propositions have some

validity to them of course, when they are explored and clarified, but to take them as they stand and regard them as a single or multiple criterion for what it means to be a Christian simply muddies the waters.

Others say that to be a Christian is to be one who does certain things, or even more often, one who does *not* do certain things, like smoking or drinking or playing golf on Sunday mornings. Strange, isn't it, that a liberating and fulfilling gospel is so often described in negative and restrictive terms. But even when it is expressed in positive terms the picture is so bland as to be indistinguishable from any normal, decent human being. So the Christian thing to do is to go to church on Sunday mornings, be kind to grandmothers and stray cats, and practice the golden rule. And the golden rule is actually a very slippery way of life, because it *can* mean that if you don't mind being slapped around, you are perfectly free to slap around anyone you choose.

Now against all that, believing certain things or doing or refraining from doing certain things, listen to Jesus on what it means to be a Christian: "I am the way and the truth and the life, no one comes to the Father, but by me." What he does say is that *he* is the way, the truth, and the life. Notice that Jesus does not say that you have to believe certain propositions about him or about God or about the Bible, nor does he say that you have to live up to certain ethical principles. And if you would come to the Father, that is, understand who and what God is and how he acts in our world today, it is "by me." Which is to say, by living and participating in the mysterious and inexhaustible love of God for us by expressing love for anyone who is in need of love—and who isn't?

The saying "No one comes to the Father, but by me" is frequently interpreted as a limiting, restrictive, exclusivistic way, interpreted by some as if Jesus were saying all other religions are wrong. But actually it is a far more liberating saying. Earlier in this passage Jesus also said, "In my Father's house are many rooms," or in the more familiar words of the King James Version, "In my Father's house are many mansions." This has usually been thought of as referring to life after death, and so it is customarily read at funerals. But it need not be so limited. It refers to the situation here and now as well. The way of love finds many forms of expression. In central Vermont, tucked away in the mountains, is a Carthusian monastery where a community of Christians spend their entire lives doing nothing but meditating and praying, praying especially for others in the world around them from which they have shut themselves off. It is one of the expressions of the way of love. You might not choose it, nor I, but they have. But on the other hand, in any large city and in a number of smaller ones there are communities of Christians who are expressing the way of love by fighting poverty and disease and inadequate housing in the law courts and at city hall—a very different expression of the way of love: "In my Father's house are many rooms." Nor need it be limited to Christian communities. As Frederick Buechner has pointed out: "It is possible to be in Christ's way and with his mark upon you without ever having heard of Christ, and for that reason to be on your way to God though maybe you don't even believe in God." "In my Father's house are many rooms."

"The way" is open ended. So Daniel Day Williams writes: "We are invited to write a new history together [that is, a new history with God, with Christ] in which the forms of love's expression cannot be identified with only one pattern or motif." And further: "We are to be prepared for the extravagance, the radical spontaneity, the unruliness of love in human existence." I like that: extravagance, spontaneity, unruliness of love. That comes so much closer to the words and spirit of Jesus than our pitiful attempts to restrict and confine the Christian way of life into a dreary list of thou shalts and thou shalt nots.

But now, although the way to which we are invited may have no set forms or patterns and may explode all over the place into a wild variety of forms and lifestyles, there is nevertheless one constant along the way. No matter how it may express itself, to follow in the way always involves suffering. The way of love that Jesus chose for himself was the way of the suffering servant, and to participate in his way is to participate in his suffering.

This is not so strange actually, since love by its very nature always involves suffering. For love makes us vulnerable. A parent, simply by the fact that he or she is a parent, faces suffering. The pain, the anguish, the loneliness of a child inevitably becomes the pain, the anguish, the loneliness of the parent. So with the lover. So with the loving husband or wife.

And so too with the broader and often deeper sufferings of the neighbor. One of the deeper impacts of *Roots* was not simply to send us off on a genealogical binge, but to enable us to enter into the sufferings of a black people in the stinking slave ships, in servile bondage on a plantation, in being bought and sold like so much cattle, and in the years of discrimination and oppression that followed, the end of which is not yet. Love makes us vulnerable. The way of Jesus, the way of love, simply means suffering. It is the way of the cross.

So what then becomes of the way of joy that Jesus talks about? "These things I have said to you that my joy may be in you and that your joy may be full." Possibly the saying points to a difference between joy and happiness. Happiness, as we usually think of it, is normally equated with the absence of pain and suffering. We speak of happiness in terms of a good vacation, a satisfying and fulfilling vocation or job, a good marriage, a happy family free from tension and illnesses, an outing to Disneyland, watching our favorite team win, spring busting out all over, a sunshiny and therefore a happy day. But joy is not that predictable. It's given to us in the presence of suffering, or perhaps more accurately, joy may be found on the other side of suffering. Not necessarily, of course. For bitterness and despair and hopelessness can also be found on the other side of suffering, as any nursing home will bear witness, and as suicide attests. But joy too can be given to us on the other side of suffering, joy in loving and being loved.

So George Matheson, blind and rejected by his beloved, sings in the familiar hymn, "O Joy that seekest me through pain, . . . I trace the rainbow through the rain, . . . And from the ground there blossoms red/Life that shall endless be."

This is not to say that the Christian seeks out suffering, or even welcomes it. Our Lord prayed passionately that the cup of suffering be taken from him; yet I have even heard some people express a vague sort of guilt because they have not suffered deeply or have been spared the kind of suffering that others have had to go through—but that way leads to morbidity. It is simply to say that the way of suffering love to which we are invited makes us vulnerable to the suffering of others even if we have been spared that kind of suffering in our own lives.

"No one comes to the Father, but by me." To be on the way to God is to know something of the love that "spared not his own

Son but delivered him up for us all." For God, as suffering love, is in this thing with us and for us.

So what does it mean to be a Christian? It has little to do with whether you belong to a church or not, though normally a Christian will want to associate with a like-minded community of people who are on the same pilgrimage. It does not necessarily mean that he or she is very far along the way. It certainly does not mean that we subscribe to one or more propositions about Jesus or God or the Bible, nor that we all look alike in our lifestyles. But a Christian is one who has accepted Jesus' invitation to pilgrimage along the way of love, sensing that out of the mystery which enfolds us, the mystery we call God, and participating in the way of love as we have seen it in the life, death, and Resurrection of Jesus, that pilgrimage will lead us to the truth and the life.

Another way of putting it is that it is a gradual change in pronouns. No longer is the *I* front and center, but rather *we* and *us*, even as our Lord taught us to pray: *Our* Father; forgive *us our* trespasses; give *us our* daily bread; lead *us* not into temptation; deliver *us* from evil. Christians are those who grow to use ever more naturally the pronouns of suffering love.

Asleep or Awake?

But as to the times and the seasons, brethren, you have no need to have anything written to you. For you yourselves know well that the day of the Lord will come like a thief in the night. When people say, "There is peace and security," then sudden destruction will come upon them as travail comes upon a woman with child, and there will be no escape. But you are not in darkness, brethren, for that day to surprise you like a thief. For you are all sons of light and sons of the day; we are not of the night or of darkness. So then let us not sleep, as others do, but let us keep awake and be sober. For those who sleep sleep at night, and those who get drunk are drunk at night. But, since we belong to the day, let us be sober, and put on the breastplate of faith and love, and for a helmet the hope of salvation. For God has not destined us to wrath, but to obtain salvation through our Lord Jesus Christ, who died for us so that whether we wake or sleep we might live with him. Therefore encourage one another and build one another up, just as you are doing. —1 Thessalonians 5:1–11

Last night I died and this morning I arose again from the dead. Almost literally! For seven or eight hours I was dead to the world, as we say. To be sure, I snored and had dreams and scratched and turned from one side to the other, but as for the world I live in, my family and friends, the work I am committed to—I was dead. Then this morning I woke up. No trumpets calling me back from the dead, no hallelujah chorus, not even a bird chorus—just the opening of the eyes, the vast urge to close them and go back to sleep again. Finally, with a consummate act of the will, I planted my feet on the floor and enjoyed my daily attack of self-righteousness because I got up. I've known some people who jump out of bed, eager to greet the new day. Not me. I can't remember a day in my life when it was not a minor triumph to rise from the death of sleep.

However your sleeping and waking habits may differ from mine, we all enact each day this familiar biblical metaphor of death and resurrection, of sleeping and waking. Paul uses it in his Letter to the Thessalonians: "But you are not in darkness, brethren, for that day to surprise you like a thief [in the night]. For you are all sons of light and sons of the day; we are not of the night or of darkness. So then let us not sleep, as others do, but let us keep awake and be sober." But not only in this passage; the Bible is full of this enacted metaphor. It frequently speaks of death as a sleep. The disciples slept while our Lord wrestled in agony in the garden. Jonah slept in the "inner part of the ship" while in flight from God's command to go to Nineveh, that great city, and prophesy. The ancient prophet of the Exile called his people to "awake, awake, put on your strength, O Zion." And in the parable of the wise and foolish bridesmaids, they were all asleep when the cry came: "The bridegroom comes. Get up and out to meet him."

Indeed the metaphor of asleep and awake is so familiar that you wonder whether there's much sense in exploring it any further, the implications are so obvious. But there are dimensions here which may be worth opening up a bit.

For one thing, even on the surface we may not be aware of how close our Christian lives and the life of the church may be to falling asleep. For me at least, one of the most delicious feelings of the day comes at night, reading in bed. The eyes no longer focus, the book slips from the hand, and you drift off to a delightful sleep. It's so much like being in church. With the soft lights and soothing music, the familiar hymns and the words of comfort and assurance, the walls closing out the noises of the world, the stained glass suggesting another world—we drift off. God's in his heaven, all's right with the world—at least for the moment. And maybe if things are not exactly all right with the world, maybe God will fix it up sometime soon without bothering me too much in the process. Sleep.

Or maybe not in church but in front of the TV screen, especially at commercial time. What a "luscious, trouble-free America" the commercials create for us: no disorders, no hunger, no crime, no poverty, no pollution; all is free from ugliness and war and trouble. It's an America filled with beautiful people, long-legged blonds, handsome western chaps in their sombreros, all tanned and well fed—a whole wonderful world. As someone has suggested, "A world of plenty: wines, fruits, breads, imported sardines, shining buildings, landscaped gardens, luscious purples, rich oranges, psychedelic swirling blues, limpid pools, and money; silvers, golds, the rich, crinkling, substantial feel of . . . bonds. All that a heart can desire . . . Now available . . . Run right down to your . . . Hurry out to your . . ." Ah, this lucious, trouble-free America. And don't blame it all on the advertisers. For if these desires in the deepest parts of our being to escape—to sleep—were not already there, the advertisers would be all washed up. Moreover most of us who watch all this have full stomachs, and it's hard to stay awake on a full stomach!

Well, with the mess the world's in, we have a right to a little escape, haven't we? "I can dream, can't I?" To be sure. The only trouble is that we might sleep right through Judgment Day. And maybe you and I would like that best of all. But Paul likens Judgment Day to a thief in the night. And then the dreams of a luscious, trouble-free America turn into nightmares. And that is just about what has happened—isn't it so? For the Day of the Lord has come like a thief in the night without our even being aware of it, bringing destruction and death. Suddenly the cities are dying, strangling to death with traffic, choking to death with smog and pollution; the lakes are dying: some have said that Erie is already dead; sparkling streams and rivers dying of filth; the streets of the cities are as empty as graveyards at night, unsafe for people to walk in; children in ghettos are bitten by rats and dying of drugs. And all of it spells Judgment Day. The Day of the Lord has indeed come like a thief in the night while we dream the dreams of a luscious, trouble-free America.

There is the sleep of escape. We're tired. The world is too much with us late and soon, and we want to get away from the mess, the problems, the demands. That's understandable, like going to sleep at night and hopefully faling into a luscious, trouble-free sleep.

But there's another kind of sleep, a rebellious sleep. Richard Luecke characterizes Jonah's sleep in the belly of the ship on the way to Tarshish as a rebellious sleep: "Why then does Jonah sleep, if not because he's tired or afraid or indifferent? The answer must be that his is a deliberate sleep, a belligerent sleep. It is a sit-down or a lie-down strike against the very conditions of human existence. Jonah has seized on the one thing he can do to resist God: he can lie there, and if God smites him he can die there, and thereby disappoint God!" This is the sleep not of the unbeliever, but of the believer. Jonah has his convictions. And "None so soundly sleep as those who sleep the sleep of the believer."

Is that too strong to characterize our sleep? Your sleep and mine? If so, then why is it so hard for us to see for example that the death of the city, like the death of Nineveh, is our responsibility? No matter whether we live in the city or the suburbs or in some small town in Tennessee or North Dakota? Why is it that though we'd be the first to defend our faith in God, we find the responsibility for the death of the city as everywhere else—in Washington or New York or Los Angeles or Chicago, in the Mayor's office or in the courts or in Congress or in police headquarters—but never in our laps? After all, what did Jonah care for Nineveh except— just like you and me—to condemn it for its sins? And when Jonah suspected that God wanted him to do something about Nineveh besides running away from it and condemning it, what did Jonah do but sleep—a rebellious, an angry sleep: God wasn't going to get Jonah involved in that mess! Jonah simply refused to acknowledge his responsibility for God's concern for Nineveh. It wasn't *his* business. Let God get somebody else. And you? And I?

So God sends what someone has called his alarm clock, Jesus, crying, "Repent for the kingdom of God is at hand." To awake from all kinds of sleep, the sleep of escape or the rebellious sleep of the believer. "Awake, awake, put on your strength, O Zion."

And that can happen too, miraculously enough. For what is this process of waking up, the rubbing of the eyes, the orange juice and coffee, the planting of the feet on the floor to face a new day? It's a miracle. Like rising from the dead. A new day. None like it ever before, and none like it will ever follow. It's a daily act of God's creation. No matter that one day seems so much like another. It's not. Each day God summons you to get up to a new life. To be sure, the old problems are still there. But there is the miracle of another day to wrestle with them, to accept them too as the gift of God.

So we are called to be awake to the same old problems: in your family, in the cities—the sickness and death, the pollution, the poverty, and all the rest of it. But that's not all. There is also the possibility of laughter and beauty and joy: in the family, in the cities, in the world. Repent, to be sure, but only because the kingdom of God is at hand. The world—your little world as well as the big world of which your little world is a part—has not slipped from God's hands.

Are you then asleep or awake? Don't try to look inside of yourself for the answer. As someone has written:

> Introspection in the long run doesn't get you very far because every time you draw back to look at yourself, you are seeing everything except for the part that drew back, and when you draw back to look at the part that drew back to look at yourself, you see again everything except for what you are really looking for. And so on. . . . In your quest to see yourself whole, (you are) doomed always to see infinitely less than what there will always remain to see. Thus when you wake up in the morning, called by God to be a self again, if you want to know who you really are, watch your feet. Because where your feet take you, that is who you are.

So the blessed alternation of sleeping and waking, for sleep too is a blessed gift of God—so long as, eyes shut or eyes open, we are not asleep all the time. For sleep brings with it not only rest and refreshment, but the closing out of the problems and perplexities and tragedies of life.

Then each morning God calls us out of that death and forgiveness to be awake again with the expectancy that our feet will take us to the place where he is, ahead of us as well as beside us, opening our eyes to the problems and perplexities of the cities and the world, to be sure, but also opening our eyes expectantly to the joy and laughter which always await us when God is in this thing with us. "Waking into the new day, we are all of us Adam on the morning of creation, and the world is ours to name."

God's Vigil

I lift up my eyes to the hills.
  From whence does my help come?
My help comes from the Lord,
  who made heaven and earth.

He will not let your foot be moved,
  he who keeps you will not slumber.
Behold, he who keeps Israel
  will neither slumber nor sleep.

The Lord is your keeper;
  the Lord is your shade
  on your right hand.
The sun shall not smite you by day,
  nor the moon by night.

The Lord will keep you from all evil;
  he will keep your life.
The Lord will keep
  your going out and your coming in
  from this time forth and for evermore.

                          —Psalm 121

"He who keeps Israel will neither slumber nor sleep." And a free translation of that might be: "You never catch God napping." That's a comforting thought in a day when the air is full of phrases suggesting that God is absent or dead. But it's a frightening thought too: you never catch God napping. Is it really so?

Every now and then in visiting churches across the countryside you run across the symbol of a single painted eye staring at you from the wall over the altar or pulpit. It has always struck me as a rather unattractive symbol, that huge, unblinking eye, utterly expressionless, staring at you no matter where you sit. It's the symbol of God's omniscience of course: sees all, knows all. Of course when you speak of it in terms of an abstraction like God's omniscience,

it's not so unsettling. But squeeze the abstraction into that unblinking eye with its relentless stare that looks right through you,
and it gives a dimension we might miss to the words of the Psalm:
"He who keeps Israel will neither slumber nor sleep."

Alan Watts has given a vivid description of the experience:

> I become aware of those Eyes watching me right through the back
> of my head—Eyes that bore implacably into the most tender and
> disreputable centers of my soul, that soon appear to surround me
> in all directions, to watch from the outside and from the inside,
> until everything is *just One Eye*. And because there is no brow,
> no face, I cannot tell what expression that Eye has. It just looks, and
> I can't stand it. I start running, running in blind panic down the
> corridors of the temple, but every way I turn I am running straight
> into that Eye. I drop to the floor, curl up, shut my eyes, and cover
> my head. Yet the Eye comes at me from deep inside me—vaster than
> ever, filling all thinkable space.
>
> There is nowhere—nowhere at all—left to go.

It is a terrifying symbol, that unblinking, all-seeing eye. Perhaps
it smacks a bit too much of "Big Brother" watching you, but let
us live with the terror for a moment.

There is no running away from it, though heaven knows we
try. Psalm 139 is the record of one man's try:

> If I ascend to heaven, thou art there!
> If I make my bed in Sheol, thou art there!
> If I take the wings of the morning and dwell
>   in the uttermost part of the sea . . .
> If I say, "Let only darkness cover me . . ."
> even the darkness is not dark to thee,
>   the night is bright as the day;
>   for darkness is as light with thee.

So you and I run too from that all-seeing eye, to the blessed
anonymity of the city perhaps, where nobody knows my name and
my privacy is undisturbed and I can get away with what I can get
away with. But there is no place to hide: city apartment, cabin in
the woods, heaven, hell, death, life, darkness, light; even that vast
bulk of self we call the subconscious, most of it lying below the
surface like an iceberg, even that is seen, known.

So in the face of that relentless eye all my pretenses come down.
All the trappings that help us put a front to the world and to
ourselves are gone: the deodorizers and perfumes which help us

smell better; the status symbols—my address, the clubs, cars, and fraternities, the people we know and don't know, the bank accounts and certificates hanging on the wall, the credit cards—all the status symbols which make me look bigger; all the good works in the community that help make me look better—PTA, den mother, community chest, hospital drives, blood campaigns—all gone. There's no retouching of the photograph of ourselves, no sword blades, magic hair curlers, or mascara to help. We are seen and known for what we really are.

And who are we really, when you strip away all the self-justification that goes on from morning till night, the games of one-upmanship we play with the neighbors and colleagues in business or at school, even with the members of our own family? That hidden, inner self even a husband does not dare show to his wife—or a wife to her husband—is seen clear through. Our privacy is public before that relentless, unblinking eye.

"He who keeps Israel will neither slumber nor sleep." Put that into the symbol of the eye, and you know what judgment is. And if you don't, then chances are you're still running, hiding, evading, justifying yourself, afraid—and I don't blame you—afraid to acknowledge the sleepless vigil of God.

But really, does all this tell you anything more than you already know? Even though we may be trying to run off and hide from it, there is something inside of us which knows that we are known, which is why we keep running, evading, excusing, pretending, playing games. This is why the rankling sense of guilt and our resort to the crumbling satisfactions of one-upmanship.

What is so difficult for you and me to accept is that the eye is not expressionless, unpitying, relentlessly judging, that life, at bottom, is not like that. Those words, "He who keeps Israel will neither slumber nor sleep," come from the Psalm which begins:

I will lift up my eyes to the hills.
    From whence does my help come?
My help comes from the Lord,
    who made heaven and earth.

He will not let your foot be moved,
    he who keeps you will not slumber.
Behold, he who keeps Israel
    will neither slumber nor sleep.

The symbol of the unblinking, expressionless eye is actually a half-truth—if that! For all that we know of that eye—really know—is what we have come to know in the life, death, and Resurrection of Christ. The eye is in the face of one whom Jesus calls, remarkably, Abba, Father. That word *Abba*, the child's name for Father, is actually the one word that we can be certain Jesus actually said.

And believe me it's no comfort to him, the Father, to see all and know all. Jesus looked at the city of Jerusalem—looked right through it to its innermost core—and wept. Imagine, for example, if we could know every thought, every secret desire, every passion and lust, every fear and deception in the hearts of even one of our children. What a comfort that we don't see them every minute of the day when they're off at school, playing along the streets; or the older ones as they conduct their private affairs at home or in the marketplace. But God, whom Jesus calls Father, knows no such comfort. The miracle that the New Testament tells about is that seeing all—and the *all*, as you let your imagination rove over all the human beings on earth, embraces everyone from ghetto and jungle to Park Avenue and Capitol Hill—he yet is willing to give his life for *all* he sees! Hosea has that unforgettable picture of God, seeing all the rebellion, the adulterous lusts for other gods in the hearts of his children, holding his hands tight behind his back and declaring, "I am God and not man, the Holy One in your midst, and I will not come to destroy."

God's unblinking eye has no interest in humiliating us just for the sake of humiliating us. Nor is he interested in comparing us with other people. "As Martin Buber once observed [of himself], in the Day of Judgment the Lord will not ask Martin Buber, 'Why were you not like Moses or Elijah?' but 'Why were you not like Martin Buber?' " This is the point of the all-seeing, unblinking eye: that we shall be willing to see ourselves for what we are, our potentialities and possibilities as well as our obvious failures. Faith in God is not so much a matter of believing something about *him*. "The basic requirement," as David Roberts has reminded us, "is not so much that I shall apprehend something as that I shall be able to stand being apprehended . . . to have courage enough to look at ourselves and to be looked at with the eye of eternity."

And what if we should be so willing to let the eyes of God see through us—what then? Well, first of all, it means that you and I are of eternal worth: worth noticing, worth looking at. And that's a burden a lot of us are reluctant to bear. It's a lot easier, really, to think of ourselves—secretly of course—as of little moment, little worth. Because then nothing is expected of us. And anything worthwhile we do happen to manage is then just so much gravy! But those eyes in the face of him whom Jesus calls Abba never let us forget that we are of eternal worth.

And I think we do need to know that! Then the seductive anonymity of the city is no longer an escape, but an opportunity. The deep yearning to be known and loved, without which we shrivel and become less than human, is satisfied, like the nostalgic refrain in Lily's haunting song, "Everybody knew my name," recalling the little village from which she had come to the carnival. For when we are known and loved, then we are free to be ourselves, what we were ultimately meant to be. The popular word today for this phenomenon of course is *acceptance*. But as Joseph Sittler has pointed out, this is not the popular kind of acceptance in our culture, when we are accepted because it makes no difference who we are or what we do, acceptance without judgment. The divine style of acceptance sees right through us and yet nevertheless—always that divine nevertheless—declares us to be of ultimate worth, which frees us to be that for which we were created, free to love, to seek justice and do mercy.

And that means that we are free from pretense, from playing games, from the daylong effort to justify ourselves to others and to ourselves. Suddenly we can see ourselves with a bit of humor and acknowledge the absurdity of our false fronts and status symbols and self-justification. Because it is absurd, isn't it? This obvious effort to prove ourselves when we obviously can't. Certainly not to those eyes which see right through us. Is it too much to suggest that there may even be a twinkle, a glint, in the eye that sees right through us when he sees us finally giving in to the absurdity of it and refusing to take ourselves so seriously in the wrong way? What else can it mean when it says, "There is joy in heaven in the presence of the angels of God over one sinner that repents"? For repentance essentially is not a woebegone, dreary business of confessing a lot of obvious faults and failures; it is the joyful release of being willing to be seen, to look at ourselves with the same unblinking realism which always is touched by a bit of humor at the absurdity of it all. And the release that brings can only be described in terms of joy. To be seen—right through—and loved at the same time. That's the miracle. And the strange part about the miracle is that we're most likely to find it to be true for ourselves when we are doing what we can to assure someone else that it is really so.

And then one thing more. This willingness to be seen by that unblinking eye in the face of the one whom Jesus calls Abba not only assures us of our worth and releases us from this constant and deadly game of pretense, but it assures us at a deeper level that whatever misfortune or tragedy—failure—we have to face and bear in life is known. God sees all that too. Not only sees it, but endures it with us; so we are assured in the life and death of our Lord. God knows precisely what it's like to be you! Helmut Thielicke uses the symbol of God's hands: nothing comes our way that has not passed through his hands. He does not ward off the tragedy and the suffering any more than he protected Jesus from it. But we can know that he looks upon it with the eye of love and compassion, and not only looks, but offers us the courage and comfort of his presence to bear and endure because he has been there too, and is there with us here and now. This is one of the things we mean when we talk about the living Christ in the Easter cycle: that Christ is alive.

So "He who keeps Israel will neither slumber nor sleep." Through the long black watches of the night, the dark hours when God seems absent, far off, or even dead, he's there—here—with you: "He will not suffer thy foot to be moved." Even as he was there with our Lord in the hour of temptation and struggle and death. It may not seem so. You may not feel it. But the Bible says very little about feelings. It declares a promise and a presence.

For you don't catch God napping. "He who keeps Israel will neither slumber nor sleep." To be sure, that can be a frightening thought, as we have seen. But all the comfort the New Testament has to offer is there too. And the comfort would be empty and cold if it did not bring with it its terror first. To be loved and not to be fully and completely known or understood or judged is small comfort. But we are seen and known—judged—by that unblinking eye. And we can face it with courage, a sense of humor, and even joy in the trust that that eye is framed by the face of one whom Jesus called Abba, Father.

How Come We Can Hear Each Other?

When the day of Pentecost had come, they were all together in one place. And suddenly a sound came from heaven like the rush of a mighty wind, and it filled all the house where they were sitting. And there appeared to them tongues as of fire, distributed and resting on each one of them. And they were all filled with the Holy Spirit and began to speak in other tongues, as the Spirit gave them utterance. Now there were dwelling in Jerusalem Jews, devout men from every nation under heaven. And at this sound the multitude came together, and they were bewildered, because each one heard them speaking in his own language. And they were amazed and wondered, saying, "Are not all these who are speaking Galileans? And how is it that we hear, each of us in his own native language? Parthians and Medes and Elamites and residents of Mesopotamia, Judea and Cappadocia, Pontus and Asia, Phrygia and Pamphylia, Egypt and the parts of Libya belonging to Cyrene, and visitors from Rome, both Jews and proselytes, Cretans and Arabians, we hear them telling in our own tongues the mighty works of God." And all were amazed and perplexed, saying to one another, "What does this mean?" But others mocking said, "They are filled with new wine." —Acts 2:1–13

The other evening on a run-of-the-mill TV dramatic show, one of the characters in the drama had been blind from birth. And from that point on you could almost write the script yourself. There was the inevitable operation, and then the drama-soaked moment when the doctor came into the room to remove the bandages from her eyes. The camera showed the dark and shadowy world of blindness slowly brightening and coming into focus, until the moment when despite ourselves tears start to well up in our eyes as the blind eyes are able to see again forms, fingers, faces.

If it is done even moderately well, that dramatic moment is all but sure fire for its effect on us. So sympathetic we are to those who are forced to live in darkness, that if by some surgical miracle sight is restored, we are all but moved to tears of joy.

Pentecost celebrates another miracle, the miracle of hearing restored. For the climax of the Pentecost experience comes not with the strange sound as of a rushing mighty wind, nor with the strange tongues as of fire resting on each of them, nor with the strange speaking with tongues "as the Spirit gave them utterance." No. The strangest thing of all was that these devout Jews, coming "from every nation under heaven," were able to hear each other! So it reads: "They were bewildered because each one heard them speaking in their own language. And they were amazed and wondered, saying, 'Are not all these who are speaking Galileans? And how is it that we hear, each of us in his own native language?' . . . And all were amazed and perplexed, saying to one another, 'What does this mean?' "

It is futile for us to ask which is the greater tragedy, blindness or deafness. Our immediate instinct, I suppose, is to count blindness the more severe. To live in a world of total darkness is horrifying to contemplate for those of us who can see, and we are overwhelmed by the courage of those who get about and even manage constructive work and family life even though blind. Deafness, on the other hand, is often regarded by those of us who can hear as almost little more than a nuisance. And yet deafness is deep tragedy too. Blindness cuts us off from things. Deafness cuts us off from people.

At least, the Bible reckons our inability to hear and understand one another as one of the great tragedies of human life. It is dramatized in the ancient story of the Tower of Babel, where as a result of man's presumptuous pride in attempting to build a tower that will reach up into the heavens so that men can be their own gods, mankind is stricken with a babel of tongues so that they are not able to understand each other. And it is this tragic inability to hear one another, to understand one another, that is miraculously healed on Pentecost. And we still are desperately in need of that miracle of healing today.

In a neighborhood where I lived in New York for a number of years, there is a large number of Spanish-speaking people. You go into the neighborhood stores on Broadway, and frequently you are surrounded by people speaking this—to me—strange and foreign language. We can smile at each other. We can be irritated by each other. But there is no basis for understanding, for really hearing each other. It is as if we lived in different worlds.

But it doesn't have to be simply a matter of speaking a language foreign to each other. There is a babel of voices all speaking the same language, and it is indeed as if we were living in different worlds. We do not hear each other. B. Davie Napier writes:

> A something quite describable is missing:
> men do not really speak to one another;
> we do not really see and read each other.
> A something sweet and soft and warm, responding
> in words, in speech, in plain communication
> is missing, wanting, absent—or illusive:
> always, O God, so damnably illusive—
> a something that is something like a Word . . .

It's missing in families. A wife, frustrated, angry, cries out to her husband, "You don't understand." And the tragedy of it is he doesn't. And when he doesn't care that he doesn't, then they are like strangers to each other: aliens, foreigners—in the same bed!

Or we call it the generation gap. But that's too pat. We avoid the tragedy by labelling it a social problem. But the tragedy runs deep when father and son, behind their age barriers, have no word, *no word* for each other that is understandable by each other. And too often the reason is as old as the story of the Tower of Babel: the stiff-necked pride on both sides which results in a confusion of tongues. God how we long for a word that will speak through the barriers of age and pride instead of insisting that the other come into my world, adopt my point of view, adopt my values, even my prejudices.

And if the problem of not being able to hear each other is present in families, it's no surprise that whites do not really hear blacks; that the affluent—you and I—do not really hear the voices of the poor, of those on relief, unemployed; that those in the suburbs and small towns do not hear—really hear—the voices in the ghettos.

Indeed the current mood among us is to raise the barriers, stop the ears rather than to open them. Affluent whites—you and I mostly—have hardened our ears. We've really given up believing in the power of Pentecost which enables strangers to hear each other. We've lost patience with that. We want to coerce, push around, punish, restrain: Bring back the death penalty. Cut welfare programs. Even Billy Graham has suggested castrating every rapist.

I know: This is understandable. Crime has gotten out of hand. Everyone feels we've got to *do* something! But what will this get-tough attitude and talk and action do to our willingness to listen to the voices crying out of the situations which breed the crime? And how in God's name will we ever come close to understanding the miracle of Pentecost, when they were bewildered and amazed that they were able to hear each other for once!

There is a movement spreading through many churches in a number of areas all over the country, sometimes called the Charismatic movement, sometimes called Pentecostalism. It is marked by healings, but above all by glossolalia, or speaking in tongues. It has appeared chiefly in Roman Catholic, Episcopalian, Lutheran, and Presbyterian churches, but it is not restricted to them of course. Those caught up in it speak of a new "baptism by the Spirit" which releases their emotions and opens them up to a direct experience of God. One of them says, "We start with a goal: an encounter with the Lord. Speaking in tongues is a tool, a means to an end, a prayer form, a childlike devotion which brings with it freedom and results in closeness to God." Given the cold formalism which marks the worship in so many churches, it is a perfectly understandable reaction. And Paul does write of speaking in tongues as one of the gifts of the Spirit.

My concern is that it not overshadow the central miracle of Pentecost which—although it included this strange speaking in tongues as well as the sound as of a rushing mighty wind and the spectacle of tongues as of fire—was that they were able to *hear* each other. When Paul lists the gifts of the Spirit, he makes it quite clear that although there are many gifts of the Spirit—healings, prophecy, faith, speaking in tongues—the greatest of these gifts of the Spirit is love.

And how could it be otherwise? If God is love, and he gives of his own Spirit to us, then that gift of himself is love: openness to each other, the ability to hear one another; then there is the miraculous possibility that the barriers of age—the generation gap—the barriers of race and class and selfishness and pride and fear can be broken down.

And how is it made possible? Through death and Resurrection. Even at the human level, death makes possible the breaking forth of the spirit of love which enables us to hear one another. When Hubert Humphrey died and those long lines of people—thousands of them—filed by the casket, they were like the crowds at Pentecost, "from every nation under heaven." There were blacks, whites, old, young, poor, rich, Republicans as well as Democrats—all, for a moment, united in their grief. So when Martin Luther King died, we were all, whites as well as blacks, open to him and to what he lived and died for: "I have a dream." How much more then has the death of Christ, followed by his Resurrection, opened us up to the miracle of Pentecost, the miracle of the baptism of the Spirit of love so that we are enabled to hear each other for once.

This does not mean that we lose our differences. I am a white, middle-class male. And presumably I will remain a white, middle-class male until I die. But if I am open to the miraculous gift of the Spirit, then I will be open to the rich differences to be found in black people, the marvelous differences in women, and the crushing differences among the poor and disadvantaged.

After all, it *is* the differences among us which love appreciates, not the sameness. When we fall in love, we do not fall in love with our common humanity. I fall in love with that which makes her different, unique: the utterly delightful idiosyncrasies of voice, movement, appearance, the way she reacts and responds—all of which belong to her alone! So on Pentecost. With the miraculous gift of the Spirit, they were in fact made even more aware of their differences. And yet despite the differences, they were able to hear each other, each in his own native language.

Please don't think of all this as a lot of idealism that I'm talking about here. This is a factual description of the way things *are*. In that old story of the Tower of Babel it is said that the whole earth had one language, symbolic of the fact that when God's creative Spirit brooded over the earth and brought forth mankind, they were created to hear one another in all of their fascinating differences. The miracle of Pentecost assures us that that creative Spirit is still at work, restlessly, eagerly trying to open us up despite ourselves, to restore us to what we were created to be: creatures able to hear and to understand each other.

"And all were amazed and perplexed, saying to one another, 'What does this mean?' But others mocking said, 'They are filled with new wine.'" They were drunk all right, but not with wine. They were drunk with the dizzying possibility of the love of God breaking out all over the place, smashing down barriers and opening our ears.

God Far—God Near

*In the year that King Uzziah died I saw the Lord sitting upon a throne,
high and lifted up; and his train filled the temple. Above him stood the
seraphim; each had six wings: with two he covered his face, and with
two he covered his feet, and with two he flew. And one called to
another and said: "Holy, holy, holy is the Lord of hosts; the whole earth
is full of his glory." And the foundations of the thresholds shook at the
voice of him who called, and the house was filled with smoke. And I
said: "Woe is me! For I am lost; for I am a man of unclean lips, and I
dwell in the midst of a people of unclean lips; for my eyes have seen
the King, the Lord of hosts!"*

*Then flew one of the seraphim to me, having in his hand a burning
coal which he had taken with tongs from the altar. And he touched my
mouth, and said: "Behold, this has touched your lips; your guilt is
taked away, and your sin forgiven." And I heard the voice of the Lord
saying, "Whom shall I send, and who will go for us?" Then I said,
"Here I am! Send me."*   —*Isaiah 6:1–8*

A student was preaching a sermon in one of my classes. When he
was through, another student reacted: "You mentioned God a lot,
but I haven't the foggiest notion of what you mean by that word
God." This is obviously symptomatic of our times. If anyone thinks
more than once about that word *God,* the questions swirl. What do
you mean by the reality behind that word *God*? What do I mean?
Is there any reality behind those three letters G–O–D? Or is it like
the grin on the Cheshire cat: the sound lingers, but what of the
reality behind the sound?

In the sixth chapter of Isaiah there is an account of one man's
stunning experience of the reality of God. It was no empty sound
drifting in the wind for him. It was an overwhelming and shatter-
ing experience which turned his whole life around. But the images
he uses to describe it—can they really help you or me in a neon-
lighted, jet-propelled, food-packaged, TV-entertained world like
ours? Thrones, seraphim with six wings, foundations shaking,

smoke, and burning coals? At first glance it may put us off. Those images are so far removed from our world, even when we're in church. How can we talk of the reality of God in our land today in terms of thrones and seraphim and smoke? It's weird. Far too far, far out.

But if we take a second look at this vision which the prophet experienced in the temple, we can see that he is saying at least two things which are essential to any understanding of the reality of God: God is far off, unapproachable, mysterious, uncontrollable; and yet, amazingly, this same unapproachable and mysterious God draws near and touches us. The throne, the seraphim with six wings, the shaking of the foundations of the temple, the smoke, the ceaseless calling out, "Holy, holy, holy is the Lord of hosts"—all this is the experience of the unapproachable, mysterious, uncontrollable, infinitely distant God. But the seraphim flying down to touch the prophet's lips with a burning coal—that is God drawing near to touch and make whole. Like a child born in a stable. Like a dying man throwing his arms against a cross on a Friday afternoon.

Many churches observe Trinity Sunday as a day for celebrating the God we have come to know as Father-Creator, the divine Son Jesus, and the Holy Spirit. But some scholars have argued—and they may have a point—that in the doctrine of the Trinity we are actually trying to say not three things about God, but two: that God is far off, beyond us, absolute and unapproachable; and at the same time that God in his beyondness draws near to us in the incarnate Son Jesus, and in the presence of the Holy Spirit. These two, the beyondness and the nearness, are always held together in tension if we are to have any understanding or experience of the God the Bible talks about, just as they are held in tension in Isaiah's vision.

But we are forever breaking that tension. At the time of the Reformation, it was God in his beyondness that had gotten out of all proportion. So Luther agonized over how he could possibly find peace or acceptance by this holy, unapproachable, mysterious, and even angry God. His momentous rediscovery of justification by grace through faith leaves us with an unpalatable and forbidding phrase, but it simply says that the awful and majestic and unapproachable God draws near to us in Christ, offering peace and forgiveness and love and hope through no efforts of our own.

Today the problem is exactly reversed. We have taken the near end of God and so embraced it as to all but suffocate his beyond-ness. Isaiah's cry in the presence of the High and Holy One, "I am a man of unclean lips, and I dwell in the midst of a people of unclean lips," is all but incomprehensible to most of us today. We say instead, "Lord, I do the best I can, you know that." Or, "Some-body upstairs must like me." Or, as a teenager put it, "I've had a groovy experience of God." Add to that our inordinate appetite for God's blessings: God bless our home and nation and schools and luncheons and church services and even our football games. The other night I saw a batter cross himself as he went up to the plate. God has almost become a kind of peripatetic blesser, like a preacher at a Rotary club.

The symptoms are evident in the way we worship. Instead of an experience of awe and wonder and mystery and glory, most churches advertise an experience of friendliness. We change the pronoun *thou*, when addressing God, to *you*. I understand the rea-sons. I do it myself on occasion. It's the revolt against archaic, Shakespearean language. But the change to the more familiar *you* is also perilous. For the *thou*, however archaic, however familiar in its original use, had come to express a sense of distance and even awe when we address the High and Holy One. Martin Buber's phrase I–thou carries more freight than I–you.

So too with our hymns: "How sweet the name of Jesus sounds in a believer's ear" comes across as soft and saccharine instead of astoundingly sweet in the presence of the High and Unapproach-able One. "Amazing grace" is no longer amazing. Is it not God's business to reassure, to forgive, and to bless? Is he not the Good Shepherd? The child in the manger?

As in worship, so in life. So in our national life: "God bless America." "In God we trust." "One nation under God." Martin Marty writes: "God is so confidently controlled that the sense of distance between his purposes and [ours] disappears. As a saying of some decades ago went:

> Gott strafe England, and God save the King.
> God this and God that, and God the other thing.
> 'Good God,' said God, 'I've got my work cut out.' "

Is it surprising that a lot of us are worried about the moral cli-mate in our country today? If God is known only in his nearness, as reassuring, blessing, loving, forgiving, then his awesome demands for integrity, honesty, justice, truth, righteousness dwindle away into a whimper. Love for the neighbor, which at rock bottom involves simple justice, respect for the integrity and freedom of others, becomes soft and sentimental. And love for the enemy is so far out as to be little more than a joke, not to be taken seriously. "God doesn't expect us to be all peaches and cream, now does he?" —or so one churchwoman once said to me.

Why should we have been so surprised at Watergate when court preachers invited to conduct the White House services could, as guests of the President, hardly do anything else but bless and reassure?

But not only in high places. If the moral climate of our time has gone soft and flabby, it has its roots in the soft and flabby morals of the majority of us. And that is tied right in with our embracing the near end of God so as to suffocate his beyondness. When the vision of the High and Holy One, unapproachable in his mystery and glory, drawing near to touch our lips with a burning coal, degenerates into mere religion, or morality tinged with emotion, or what a man does with his solitude, then, writes C. S. Lewis, that flabby kind of religion "is not good at saying No."

Frederick Buechner suggests that we cannot really stand to hear the full message of the Bible anymore, like the story of Noah and God's terrible despair over the human race:

> We do not want to read it, or at least do not want to read it for what it actually says, and so make it instead into a fairy tale, which no one has to take seriously—just the way we make black jokes about disease and death so that we can laugh instead of weep at them; just the way we translate murder and lust into sixth-rate television melodramas, which is to reduce them to a size that anybody can cope with; just the way we take the nightmares of our age, the sinister, brutal forces that dwell in the human heart threatening always to overwhelm us, and present them as the Addams family or the monster dolls that we give, again, to children. *Gulliver's Travels* is too bitter about man, so we make it into an animated cartoon. *Moby Dick* is too bitter about God, so we make it into an adventure story for boys. Noah's ark is too something-or-other else, so it becomes a toy with a roof that comes off so you can take the little animals out.

Is there then any way by which we can restore the tension

between the unapproachable High and Holy One and the one who draws near? Any way to get out of this suffocating obsession with God's nearness?

Well first we have to soak ourselves in the primary realization that God is mystery, and from our human point of view unknowable. As another puts it: "When all is said and done, God is still *incognitus* [unknown] and *absconditus* [far off]. Only through the biblical revelation do we know of a God of grace and mercy, whom we worship in faith. For the Christian, this God is most meaningfully present to us in Jesus Christ. But God himself is unknowable. . . . At most we can but hold an attitude of reverent agnosticism regarding his inner nature."

That may very well be true. But can we actually experience the beyondness as well as the nearness anymore? For we cannot experience the nearness—can we?—unless we experience the beyondness! As for me, it does come sometimes in worship, and most especially when I go forward to receive the bread and wine and they touch my lips—like a burning coal. With the singing of the Sanctus, the song of Isaiah's seraphim, "Holy, holy, holy is the Lord of hosts; the whole earth is full of his glory," I am frequently touched by an experience of the mystery of God, the High and Holy One, unapproachable in glory, bending down to touch me in love and reassurance and hope through bread and wine. The mystery both of his beyondness and of his nearness comes alive for me.

But outside of formal worship? Yes. I think it is still possible for you and for me to be aware of the beyondness of God, of his distance, of his unapproachableness, of his mystery. When we're alone perhaps. And the masks we wear most of the time drop off. And I wonder about me. And the future. Is there any future? Any real future? And I wonder about the senselessness of life, its brutalities, its terrors. *Deus absconditus*. God, if there is a God, far off. Inscrutable. Awareness of distance. Infinite distance. Or perhaps not physically alone. In a New York subway. Surrounded by hordes of people. Yet nobody knows me. Nobody knows my name. Does anybody know me or my name? And what about those hordes of people? Millions of them in New York City, or infinitely more millions of them in India . . . China . . . Russia . . . Africa. Can there possibly be a God who knows them? Each one by name? Cares about each one by name? *Deus absconditus.* God far, far off. The stranger in his distance, in his beyondness.

Then, perhaps, the miracle. It is this stranger, unknown and unknowable, far off, distant, unapproachable, apparently uncaring much of the time, who draws near in Christ to touch my lips, your lips, with a burning coal.

Someone has suggested that "whenever the people of God have been caught up by an awareness of the awful holiness of God, or even the distance of God" it is the work of the Holy Spirit drawing near to remind us of the tension. "When we are taken up by the sense of the terrible other-ness of God, or let's say the sense that he is far beyond us and beyond our control, then we have been visited by the Holy Spirit."

So the tension is retained. God in his nearness—when we are actually open to God in his nearness, incredibly reaching across a great chasm, a great gulf—makes us conscious of his otherness, of his distance. Then the name of Jesus indeed sounds sweet in our ears. Then "amazing grace" is, by God, amazing!

Only as Isaiah experienced *both* the mysterious, terrible other-ness of God *and* the nearness of God was he enabled to hear the voice of God speaking directly to him: "Whom shall I send, and who will go for us?"

The authentic voice of God addressed to you, whether in demand—"Go love"—or in reassurance—"Come unto me you that labor and are heavy laden"—can be heard only as it is experienced as coming from both God far and God near. Any other voice, heard *only* as inordinate demand as with Luther in his early days, or heard *only* as suffocating comfort and reassurance as with many of us today, is spurious. It is a demonic distortion of the God who speaks to us in the Bible. Indeed it is an idol of our own devising.

Maybe, just maybe, as a crisis in the world of Isaiah—"the year that King Uzziah died"—cracked him open to the possibility of a vision of the High and Holy One, so today the crises in our world in recent years—Southeast Asia, Watergate, inflation, pollution, crime, the agony in the Middle East, hunger—may crack us open too to the possibility of an experience of God far off, unapproachable in his awesome and holy glory, *and* to the miracle of that same God bending down to touch our lips with a burning coal and make us whole.

Love—Spontaneous or Measured?

Once when great crowds were accompanying him, he turned to them and said: "If anyone comes to me and does not hate his father and mother, wife and children, brothers and sisters, even his own life, he cannot be a disciple of mine. No one who does not carry his own cross and come with me can be a disciple of mine. Would any of you think of building a tower without first sitting down and calculating the cost, to see whether he could afford to finish it? Otherwise, if he has laid its foundation and then is not able to complete it, all the onlookers will laugh at him. 'There is a man,' they will say, 'who started to build and could not finish.' Or what king will march to battle against another king, without first sitting down to consider whether with ten thousand men he can face an enemy coming to meet him with twenty thousand? If he cannot, then, long before the enemy approaches, he sends envoys, and asks for terms."   —Luke 14:25-32 (NEB)

You know, every time I think I have God, or life, pretty well figured out and I start rummaging through the Bible, then—ZAP! Some new shaft of light shatters my neat little God-package or life-package. My cozy figuring out is undercut or deflated, and I've got to take a fresh look at the whole business again.

Of course if this didn't happen the Bible would have no authority for us. It would not convey a word from the beyond at all; it would simply be a dull, commonplace book, handy to have around to confirm me in my prejudices and partial understandings. For if this Bible is in any sense a word of God, then by its very nature it has to startle and surprise, shake us up. It just won't let me spell life, or God, with the letters of *my* alphabet.

A case in point are the two little parables in the fourteenth chapter of Luke about a man building a tower and a king planning warfare:

Would any of you think of building a tower without first sitting down and calculating the cost, to see whether he could afford to finish it? Otherwise, if he has laid its foundation and then is not able to complete it, all the onlookers will laugh at him. 'There is the man,' they will say, 'who started to build and could not finish.' Or what king will march to battle against another king, without first sitting down to consider whether with ten thousand men he can face an enemy coming to meet him with twenty thousand? If he cannot, then, long before the enemy approaches, he sends envoys, and asks for terms.

So what's so surprising about all that? Isn't this just ordinary folk wisdom, hard business sense, sound military strategy? The boardroom of a big corporation, with sound business heads deciding on expansion on the basis of costs, earning capacity, and the state of the economy? Or the high strategy session in the Pentagon, with colonels and generals figuring out every deployment, the state of the military budget, and probable body-count? Or a family sitting down to decide whether they can manage the mortgage payments on a new house? No, there's nothing very surprising here; it's just plain horse sense to count up the cost before making a venture.

What is surprising is what it does to a totally different approach to discipleship, to the expression of love, in so much of the New Testament where the emphasis is just the opposite of this prudent, cautious, cost-counting approach. It's the magic, the wonder of love offered spontaneously, freely, with abandon. How many times shall I forgive—seven times? No, seventy times seven. If a man forces you to go one mile, go with him two. If he strikes you on the right cheek, offer him the left, and if he wants your corduroy jacket, offer him your topcoat too. If you love those who respond to you in friendship and love, so what? Love your enemies where you can count on nothing in return. If the wine at the wedding feast runs low, I'll drown them in more wine than they can possibly drink. And who ends up in outer darkness? The one-talent man who was precisely the cautious, prudent, counting-the-cost kind of guy.

So Jesus lived, apparently, with an abandon of love, scattering his seed over all kinds of ground, not counting the cost of scattering seed on beaten paths, on rocks, or among weeds. So he went about offering his love to every Tom, Dick, and Harry: prostitutes, call girls, racketeers, blind beggars, and God knows what all! The spontaneity of it, the uncalculating spirit, the generosity of it—this is what gives it its magic and its wonder, and draws us to him.

And occasionally it happens among us too I suppose. Sometimes in very small ways. A spur-of-the-moment phone call arrives when you're lonely or depressed, just to let you know someone's thinking of you. Or sometimes in larger ways: a decision to join Vista or the Peace Corps, to give a part of your life anyway, to help those who may need what you have to give. It's the spontaneous, uncalculating expression of love, of care for others, which seems closest to the spirit of Christ and gives life much of its wonder, magic, and joy.

At least that's the way I thought I had it all figured out. That it is precisely this delightful spontaneity, this *not* counting the cost, which is of the essence of Christian love, of the way God would have it happen among us.

So what goes on here all of a sudden with the calculating bit? The ridicule heaped on the tower builder who had not counted the cost and wasn't able to finish? Or the king waging warfare who was commended because he was willing to compromise when he found he was outmanned by the opposition? Good God, isn't it better to venture love even if we can't carry through on it? Isn't it better to fight for love and justice in our world even if we know that the opposition will probably shoot us down? At least this is the quality which draws us to make heroes of some of the Christians in our time, from Bonhoeffer, shot down by the Nazis, to Martin Luther King, shot down in his battle against white racism.

So what goes on here? Well, for one thing, Jesus suggests that the spontaneous offer of love may well be no more than an emotional kick, an expression of feelings, *our* feelings, rather than considering the effect those feelings may have on others. You recall that incident along the road where a woman, all carried away with her emotions, blurted out to Jesus, "How blessed for a mother to have a son like you!" To which Jesus replied tartly, "Yes, rather, blessed are they who hear the word of God and keep it." He was not about to let that woman get away with an outburst of feelings without counting the cost of what it did mean for Mary to have such a son, with the sword piercing her soul down through the years.

Obviously the blacks know a great deal more about this than any of us white liberals—the spontaneous offer of love and justice which lacked the guts or the imagination to follow through.

And a lot of us, to be frank, fighting for years now for a better break for the blacks, are getting sick of it! Isn't it so? The issues are so complicated, the results so problematic—along with the increase of muggings and burglaries and all the rest of it! We'd like our streets and homes to be safe! Right?

Jesus is saying in these two little parables that there is something demonic about love that does not count the cost and, having counted the cost, carry through on it. No doubt this is why Luke places these little stories in the context of that harsh demand: "If anyone comes to me and does not hate his father and mother, wife and children, brothers and sisters, even his own life, he cannot be a disciple of mine." To say Jesus is indicating that love for the neighbor immediately establishes priorities is not to water down his word one bit: those priorities can be devastating to our normal way of living!

Paul Monka in his delightful little book *Meditations in Universe*, which is full of remarkable insights into our situation both human and divine, has one clinker when he writes: "All's well that means well." Nothing could be farther from what our Lord is getting at here. The world is full of grief and loneliness and tragedy because of people like you and me who meant well but didn't count the cost. The tragedy of the blacks in this country results not alone from the arrant racists, prejudiced and bigoted, but from a hundred years and more of white people like you and me who meant well. The tragedy remains because we still haven't faced up to the cost of it all! God help the neighbor if our love for him begins and ends simply with our feelings for him.

Beyond that, these little parables suggest that love had better take sharp stock of the nature, quality, and size of the opposition. We'd better know what we're up against, and what we're up against is the monumental tragedy in human life, as well as human perversity—or evil, or sin, if you'd rather. All in all, that is awesome opposition. Which is why the basic ingredient in the biblical understanding of love, whether divine or human, is not the feeling of love, but faithfulness. It is God's *faithful* love which is asserted over and over again in the Old Testament. And when Job and others questioned the love of God for them, it was the faithfulness of that love in times of suffering and death which was in question. And in the New Testament it is the faithfulness of love even unto death which is central.

So in the Christian marriage ceremony we do not pledge our feelings of love, we pledge to each other our *troth*, an old-fashioned word for our faithfulness in sickness and in health, for better for worse. And as for friendship, you know from your own experience it is the faithful ones, those who stick by no matter what, who are the treasured ones. Others may be more fun to be with, more charming, but, by God, when the chips are down it's the faithful ones we are grateful for, even if they happen to be pretty dull customers.

Rollo May points out the need for faithfulness in love by contrasting it with the hippie movement.

> Hippie love emphasizes immediacy, spontaneity, and the emotional honesty of the temporary moment. . . . The immediacy, spontaneity, and honesty of the relationship experienced in the vital *now* are sound and telling criticisms of contemporary bourgeois love and sex. . . . But love also requires enduringness. Love grows in depth by virtue of the lovers experiencing encounter with each other, conflict and growth, all over a period of time. These cannot be omitted from any lasting and viable experience of love.

The hippies have reminded us of that which many of us have lost, the wonder and magic of love's spontaneity. But without enduringness or faithfulness, it droops and fades.

I suppose we can sum it all up by saying, as Dietrich Bonhoeffer points out, that God defines love; love does not define God. And as God defines love, it is *both* spontaneous, free, uncalculating, given with abandon *and* at the same time prudent, cautious, aware of the cost and the opposition. And somehow we have to learn to keep one without losing the other.

The old, old story of the Good Samaritan still tells it best: There was the spontaneous and immediate seizure of the moment, the now, in response to the poor guy in the ditch beside the road. But that was not all. He counted the cost, picked him up, set him on his donkey, took him to the inn, and saw to it that he was cared for. He saw it through. Both spontaneity and faithfulness.

My mother liked to contrast her two sons when we were young. I, she said, on being asked to do some chore or errand, would brightly answer yes, and then not carry through. My brother would often grumble and say no, but then do it.

If we have to sacrifice one for the other, faithfulness is more to be desired than spontaneity. Love without spontaneity can of course be dull and drab, pedestrian. But love without faithfulness is chaotic, if not demonic. But when both are held together—the instant feeling of compassion, the warmth, the spontaneity, *plus* the counting the cost and following through—then we are defining love as God defines it, not spelling it by the letters of our own alphabet.

"Follow Me"

As Jesus passed on from there, he saw a man called Matthew sitting at the tax office; and he said to him, "Follow Me." And he rose and followed him.

And as he sat at table in the house, behold, many tax collectors and sinners came and sat down with Jesus and his disciples. And when the Pharisees saw this, they said to his disciples, "Why does your teacher eat with tax collectors and sinners?" But when he heard it, he said, "Those who are well have no need of a physician, but those who are sick. Go and learn what this means, 'I desire mercy, and not sacrifice.' For I came not to call the righteous, but sinners." —Matthew 9:9–13

We've had more than our share of pious chatter in pulpits and elsewhere about "following Jesus," until the phrase has often become an embarrassment. But, trouble is, you can't avoid wrestling with the fact and implications of "follow me," because that's how the whole business got started in the first place.

Jesus, that wandering rabbi-healer-teacher-rebel, had not got very far along before he went up to this one and that—James, John, Peter, and others—and said, "Follow me." And they did. So here with Matthew. Matthew was in his office on the third floor of Seventh Avenue and Forty-ninth Street, minding his own business, bending over tax form XL259, when Jesus apparently walked in and said, "Follow me." And Matthew got up and did just that. A very strange circumstance.

So Matthew was called to pilgrimage, like Bunyan's Pilgrim or, more recently and more familiarly, like Alice in *Through the Looking Glass* or Dorothy in the Land of Oz. And surely today it must seem just as fanciful, much like a fairy story. Follow Jesus into IBM or GE or DuPont, into the Pentagon or stock exchange or TV studio, into the supermarket or factory or filling station?

Does it ever really happen today? Can it? Or do we have to leave it forever in the outlandish costumes of Sunday school pageants? Follow Jesus—is there any reality left in that phrase here at all? Can you picture it, for yourself for example?

Or, to move back a bit, how would it sound? "Follow me." Whose voice today?

For Matthew we assume it must have been easy. There he was— Jesus of Nazareth, who else? And then we're tempted to explain Matthew's response in psychological terms: the pull of Jesus' terrific personality, or perhaps his obvious authenticity. But maybe it would be better to recall that for Matthew the person of Jesus was at least as problematic as for us, and probably more so. An itinerant preacher walks in and says, "Follow me," and on the spot Matthew throws over a lucrative racket for a gigantic question mark. What sense does it make?

But whose voice today? We talk a little too glibly about the living Christ. Have you ever heard his voice? Unmistakably? Most of us have heard no inner voices, seen no visions like Paul on the Damascus road. We hear a plethora of voices saying "Follow me": Jimmy Carter, George Meany, Billy Graham, Mao Tse-tung, and parents too innumerable to mention. How do we know which carries the voice of Jesus? If any?

Traditionally the church has associated the voice with baptism, most frequently, I suppose, at an age when it obviously made no sense to us. But so it came to me, as I was led to understand later through parents, Sunday-school teachers, professors of theology, and others. Until I reached a point where the whole business began to fall apart, and I came to look upon baptism along with everything else—Bible, church, catechism, the whole bit—as an older generation's put-on, and I wanted out.

But as you grow there are a plethora of voices, many of them within the church. Some of us have heard them: "Look buddy, you have a talent or two the church could use. Why not?" Are these the voices of the authentic "follow me"? Outside the churches it's a welter of voices coming from every miserable spot on the face of the earth: Harlem ghetto, Mississippi Delta, Appalachian mountain cabin, children in South Africa—you name it, the voice of crying need. Is that the voice of Jesus saying, "Follow me"?

Most of us today assume so—if there is a voice like his at all in our world. But is simply the voice of desperate human need the voice of Jesus? Before you come up with a quick and easy "Of course," think of all the human need Jesus made no effort to meet: the sick he did not heal, the slaves he did not set free, the poor he did not reach, the hungry he did not feed. When presumably he could have. For in addition to meeting physical need, he went about preaching, of all things! And so did the disciples.

His voice obviously includes the voice of crying human need, but it is more. For Matthew presumably there was more. Certainly it was a voice that offered the promise of meaning and purpose to *his* life, Matthew's life. Beyond the human voice of Jesus, a mysterious pushing and pulling as if to indicate that here, *here*, in following Jesus, is the clue to the whole confusing stuff of life and death.

So today, beyond the plethora of specific voices of need, comes a haunting voice out of the mystery saying that this is what life's all about: "Follow me." And some of us can now look back on our baptism as signifying this amazing grace of God which singles me out before I can even know it or be aware of it, and I can say yes, there was a voice coming to me out of the mystery, saying, "Follow me."

So maybe within and beyond the specific human voices, from whatever source, we hear the voice: "Follow me"—the invitation to pilgrimage. What equipment is necessary then for pilgrimage? What sacrifices? After all, Jesus did say we would have to count the cost. What motivation?

To be sure, Matthew gave up a lucrative racket. But apparently there was no cleaning-up necessary, no psychological examination of his motives, no questionnaire to fill out or pledge cards to sign. Jesus took this rather unlikely prospect for the Kingdom and simply said, "Come along." And maybe that's as good a place as any for us to begin.

As we follow along, there will be decisions to be made, hard decisions, sacrifices to be made, but at the start there's little sense in navel-gazing as to whether our motives are beyond reproach. After all, if that were so no one, including Matthew, could get up and go at all.

I suppose the motives that lead young people to enter the Peace Corps or Vista, or to study medicine or law or theology or social work, are as mixed as anyone's. Part of it, no doubt, is to be useful, but part may be to get out of a family rut or to see the world or to be known as someone who is doing something interesting— *exciting,* as the word of the moment has it. Since most of us, as someone has put it, are "seldom less than nine parts fake," let's forget about all this motivation business and get on with it. The familiar charge of hypocrisy, levelled I suppose most frequently at the older generation, has a hollow ring no matter in whose mouth it is heard.

Nor are we required to adopt a particular set of moral standards or adhere to a given lifestyle, though that may come later in any number of patterns. As Günther Bornkamm has written: "The special demand made upon the disciples . . . must not be understood at all as a moral code for an elite, as a proclamation of an ascetic ideal which Jesus exacts only from the few."

To be sure, the one who hears the voice is called upon to be humble: "The pupil is not above his master." But one of the familiar beatitudes throws light on the surprising quality of humility. When Jesus says, "Blessed are the meek," that word *meek* in the original was the word used for wild chariot horses trained to bit and bridle. All the raw spirit, enthusiasm and spontaneity and individuality remain—so long as it is in the service of the one we follow.

This tempers our judgment as to whether there really is such a thing as an identifiable Christian look or lifestyle. There is room for all sorts and kinds of lifestyles, from revolutionary social activism to the mousy little woman who spends her time visiting the sick and elderly within a block of her mousy little home.

Is there any single lifestyle which can be called Christian? Or more Christian than others? Some have tomato juice before dinner; others have a glass of wine or beer, or a martini. Some have a scotch and water before going to bed; others gorge themselves on apple pie and coffee, or ice cream and cake. Some protest and march and picket; others work quietly with their families and neighbors in the community. Some were drafted a few years ago and went willingly to Southeast Asia; others burned their draft cards and went to prison in protest against the war. Is any one more Christian than another?

As one student said, "Jesus is cool, man, cool! When are you Christians going to figure it out?"

One of the blights suffered by the church is the assumption that every Christian's lifestyle must look alike—usually a reflection of our own. But God loves us too much to destroy the delightful individuality each one of us has. The only thing that is the same for all of us is that we are loved and are called to love, and love is indeed a many-splendored thing! You can't pour it all into the same bottles with the same labels. If you do, it will get stale and tasteless—or explode!

And if all this is true at the start, a mixed bag of motives and widely varying lifestyles, it is no less true after we have followed along for a while. The careers of the disciples who got up and left the unfinished tax forms or fishing nets or whatever are checkered, to say the least. Studded with denials, betrayals, questionable ambition, desertion under pressure, wanting to call down God's wrath on unfriendly villages, it reads for all the world like a sociologist's report of a congregation in Middletown, U.S.A. The one thing those early Christian followers did do was to pick up the pieces and follow along again.

As Frederick Buechner has described it: "We always answer with our feet. We get up and start following. Or we do not. Maybe we just plant our feet squarely in the ground and pretend we did not hear. Or we move them all right, but in another direction." But if we do decide to follow, we follow with our feet, which may lead us into libraries or slums or hospitals or nursing homes or law courts or schools or fields or churches or wherever it is that we think we hear the voice most clearly. It would be nice to think that we follow wholeheartedly, with full heart and mind and will—"total commitment" and all that—and maybe a few can manage it. Most of us, like the disciples, are less saintly. Our feet drag many a morning, and we wonder why in God's name we ever thought we heard a voice. But if the feet keep following . . .

And if the feet keep following, then what? Well, they lead us into a Christian community of some kind, and not one of our choosing. Matthew did not shop around for a community that would suit him and his particular interests, where his children would meet suitable companions, where the atmosphere and the people would be congenial to his tastes, to his revolutionary outlook—or to his conservative outlook. As a matter of fact, the first community Matthew was called into, the twelve disciples, included Simon the Canaanite, a Zealot, a revolutionary who hated the guts of guys like Matthew who played footsie with the despised Romans.

Many among the youth today have all kinds of hang-ups about "following Jesus" because in the minds of some to follow Jesus means associating with an institutional church which turns their stomachs. Of course there are always some who want to form a new, ideal Christian community composed of like-minded, authentic human beings, as the phrase goes, free of hypocrisy and cant, committed to involvement of a specific kind or to a prescribed kind of lifestyle. And yet the history of the church is studded with attempts to establish more authentic Christian communities, and they have all ended up as just another establishment, just one more denomination or sect.

This is not to downgrade experimental Christian communities, but it is to say that the first Christian community took people exactly as they were—Matthew, Peter, John, Judas—and the one thing which held them together at all was a common commitment to follow with their feet, with no prescriptions as to just how those feet were to move.

And beyond that? The destination? Who knows? Through the Looking Glass? The Land of Oz? The Kingdom of God? The place where we are needed, obviously. And that may not be where we think we'd like to be needed. It may be Jerusalem, citadel of the establishment. Or unfriendly villages, or oven more unfriendly cities . . . Corinth, Chicago, Ephesus, Cleveland.

But even beyond the places where we are obviously needed, those who followed were to be "fishers of men" in the quite unpleasant sense of "hooking them": calling them into the same pilgrimage.

After all, it was love for Matthew which said, "Follow me," as well as love for others in need of food and health and love . . . and along with that, the loving passion to bring others into submission to and acceptance of that love. The voice—in whatever accent you may hear it—speaks from love to love, that others may hear the voice of love: "Follow me."

Gifts and the Giver

On the way to Jerusalem he was passing along between Samaria and Galilee. And as he entered a village, he was met by ten lepers, who stood at a distance and lifted up their voices and said, "Jesus, Master, have mercy on us." When he saw them he said to them, "Go and show yourselves to the priests." And as they went they were cleansed. Then one of them, when he saw that he was healed, turned back, praising God with a loud voice; and he fell on his face at Jesus' feet, giving him thanks. Now he was a Samaritan. Then said Jesus, "Were not ten cleansed? Where are the nine? Was no one found to return and give praise to God except this foreigner?" And he said to him, "Rise and go your way; your faith has made you well." —Luke 17:11–19

Someone has suggested that "humanity is like an enormous spider-web, so that if you touch it anywhere, you set the whole thing trembling."

One place where this enormous spiderweb is set a trembling constantly is in the common, everyday experience of saying, "Thank you" and "You're welcome." We do it ten—a hundred—times a day as we touch another's life or another's life touches ours. Usually we do it so casually that the implications of the ordinary words of gratitude and response escape us.

Underneath the casual words there is a deep urge within us to be grateful and to express it. Someone holds a door for us, a waitress serves a drink, the driver of a car amazingly holds up so that we can break through the line, and we are grateful, because this is the way life should be—full of courtesy and thoughtfulness, reminders that we are all dependent on each other. And we respond casually, but actually out of the depths of our being: "Thank you." Of course if someone is thoughtless or rude we can use the same words in anger: "Well, thank you for that." Which is a way of crying out against the lack of recognition that we are all dependent upon each other.

When it comes to receiving thanks, we are more ambivalent.

Paul Tillich points out that the casual response to expressions of gratitude—"You're welcome," or the German *Bitte,* "Please"—indicates a certain reluctance to accept thanks. This reluctance is expressed most forthrightly in the frequent response, "Don't mention it." It indicates, I suppose, a reluctance on our part to have others dependent upon us rather than our being dependent upon others. The very uncertainties in these common expressions of gratitude and our responses to them indicate our ambivalence with respect to the enormous spiderweb of humanity, our basic interdependence upon each other. Frequently we want to withdraw entirely. As we say so often, "I really don't want any thanks." I wonder why? Because we do, really. There's a vacuum, a feeling of emptiness, when in response to some kindness or thoughtfulness of ours, no thanks are forthcoming.

Well all this is involved—and more—in the story of the healing of the ten lepers, when only one returned to give thanks to Jesus and praise to God for the miraculous gift of health. You wonder whether Jesus had these ambivalent feelings about giving thanks and receiving it. After all, wasn't it enough for the nine lepers who did not return simply to feel overwhelmingly grateful and to go off and share their joy with friends and relatives? No doubt they were having a ball! It almost sounds grudging, this disappointment over the fact that only one returned to give thanks. Isn't it enough for God to give health and joy to people? Isn't it love at its best when it desires no thanks for it? How come this need on the part of God for thanks and praise for his love? It almost begins to sound small.

Maybe that's why a lot of people today, both Christian and non-Christian, continue to leave church and churchgoing out of their lives. Many of them are obviously grateful, some of them overwhelmingly grateful, for life and joy and energy and gifts. The gratitude is spontaneous, free from restraints, free from the forced kind of gratitude expressed in most prayers of thanksgiving offered in church.

Moreover there is always the risk of dishonesty in these preplanned and formal prayers of thanksgiving in which everyone present is expected to join. Are we always to be grateful, no matter what? Suppose that you've just learned that you have terminal cancer, or that your wife has been killed in an automobile accident —are you to be grateful for that? Maybe—just maybe—at some future time you can find it inside of yourself to be grateful again, but at the time? Piety too often degenerates into dishonesty. And the biblical writers were above all utterly honest with God. "Out of the depths the psalmist *cries* to God; he does *not* thank him." Jeremiah curses the day he was born. Job argues with God in the face of the calamities which fell on him; he does not thank God for them. Are we supposed to give thanks to God always and for everything?

So why this disappointment on Jesus' part when only one leper returned to give thanks and praise to God? Well, for one thing, a marvelous and miraculous cure had been given to them, not a calamity. And Jesus was concerned that there be recognition of the Giver behind the gift. A person can rejoice in gifts, as did the other nine no doubt, and as we do all the time when good things come our way. But Jesus was concerned that they recognize their dependence upon the Giver for all the good they had experienced in life— for we come into this life naked, bringing nothing, and we leave this life naked, taking nothing away. Otherwise, if we rejoice only in the gifts, then we tend to view those gifts as a right. As something we earn or deserve. No doubt the nine lepers said to each other and to their friends and relatives, "Well it's about time!" This is God's business, isn't it? To heal and restore? To give joy and delight? It's about time that God was about his proper business.

And from there it's only a short step to the point where we think the only religion worth having is a religion that works. And that demonic attitude is always sniffing at the heels of all of us, and sometimes not even sniffing but blatantly coming at us in advertisements in pious magazines: Here is a religion that works! If I read the Bible every day, say my prayers, go to church, then good things are bound to happen to me sooner or later. If the gifts are at the center of things, then we are back in one of the most ancient forms of idolatry. We are in no better shape than the ancient Jews going a whoring after the Baals, the fertility gods. Their stock-in-trade was the gifts, of course: seeds and growth and germ cells, and birth and procreation and abundant crops and herds.

And what's the difference between that kind of idolatry and the kind of idolatry which will use God to get whatever gifts we may have in mind: peace of mind; or spiritual gifts of an esoteric kind, like speaking with tongues; or the gift of health; or the urge to have the *feeling* of God's presence; or to be given some incontrovertible proof of life after death, whether through the cult of reincarnation or whatever? If our religion works, if the fact that it works for us is the major test of its validity, then we are testing God, and he's at the end of our string, to pull in whatever direction we may see fit. Then we are at the center of life, not God.

So . . . "Was no one found to return and give praise to God except this foreigner?" Jesus was concerned that priority be given to the Giver rather than to the gifts. Otherwise there can be no spontaneity in thanksgiving, no inward joy, no possibility of ever being surprised by joy.

Moreover suppose the gifts are withdrawn. What then? To whom do you turn then, when there are no gifts to celebrate? All of us go through times of tragic loss. I have had mine and you have had yours. When life fell in on us. With tragic suddenness. There we were, overwhelmed by grief and loneliness and remorse. And at the moment, at least, there are no discernible gifts to celebrate, no life to celebrate. What then? By God, that's the time when you turn to the Giver in trust and hope that something new can be resurrected from the ashes. No proof of his presence then. No feeling of his presence then. Then, like Job, you simply hang in there: "Even though he slay me, yet will I trust him."

A run-down New York hotel, long overdue for demolition, is still inhabited by a handful of elderly people living there alone since there's no place else available which they can afford. One seventy-five-year-old resident, a woman hospitalized with Parkinson's disease who had no other neighbors or friends, pleaded to be sent "home" from the hospital to her shabby little room in that dilapidated hotel. "On her bedside table was a tiny figure of Santa Claus, and beside her on the bed was a child's stuffed animal, worn with hugging." When the bottom falls out of life, what then?

But suppose the gifts are not totally withdrawn. Then giving praise to God the Giver consecrates the gifts. In the First Letter to Timothy it is written: "For everything created by God is good, and nothing is to be rejected if it is received with thanksgiving; for then it is consecrated by the word of God and prayer." The life of the despised Samaritan, who returned to give thanks and praise, was consecrated as the lives of the other nine were not, delighted as they may have been with the gift of health. So this despised

Samaritan's life became holy in a way the lives of the other nine Jews were not. For gifts that are consecrated in thanks and praise to God become bearers of grace. Therefore we say "grace" when we give thanks for the food set before us.

So holiness enters into the secular world through the consecration of God's gifts in thanksgiving to him. For those of you who find this deep chasm between faith and life, between what goes on in church and what goes on in the world outside of church, this demonic split between the sacred and the secular, here is one first and indispensable step: thank the Giver for the gift—of life, of healing, of joy, of employment, of skills—and thus consecrate it. For thus does the holy enter into the secular world.

Thus may the enormous spiderweb of humanity be set a tremble once again, not merely from the touch of life with life, expressing our dependence upon each other, but from the touch of life with the Giver of life, expressing our dependence upon him. So Jesus said to this grateful Samaritan, as he also says to us, "Rise and go your way; your faith has made you well."

Getting God off Your Back

Bel bows down, Nebo stoops,
   their idols are on beasts and cattle;
these things you carry are loaded
   as burdens on weary beasts.
They stoop, they bow down together,
   they cannot save the burden,
   but themselves go into captivity.

"Hearken to me, O house of Jacob,
   all the remnant of the house of Israel,
who have been borne by me from your birth,
   carried from the womb;
even to your old age I am He,
   and to gray hairs I will carry you.
I have made, and I will bear;
   I will carry and will save."
                              —Isaiah 46:1–4

There are more glints of humor in the Bible than we are usually aware of, probably because we don't take the Bible seriously enough, which is to say, read it for what it says rather than reading our own notions of ponderous piety into it. In Second Isaiah, for example, there is this picture of idolatry which is ludicrous, ridiculous—at least the writer so intended it: "Bel bows down, Nebo stoops,/ their idols are on beasts and cattle;/ these things you carry are loaded/ as burdens on weary beasts./ They stoop, they bow down together,/ they canot save the burden,/ but themselves go into captivity."

The setting is Babylon, with Cyrus the Persian bearing down, about to capture the fabulous city. And where are the gods of Babylon who are supposed to save and protect against such catastrophes? In a panic, two of the leading gods of the Babylonian pantheon, Bel and Nebo, are loaded on donkeys, their noses trailing in the dust, in a futile and ridiculous attempt to save them from the conquering Cyrus.

The humor is not particularly subtle. It's the broad, slapstick humor of anything pretentious getting knocked off its pedestal, like a top hat by a snowball, or like a preacher I once knew who, reading the committal service at a cemetery in the rain, slipped right down in the mud into the open grave as he was intoning, "Earth to earth." It's slapstick. So here, in the face of a crisis, the magnificent gods of Babylon are ignominiously carted off in cringing safety on weary beasts.

But I suppose the exiles did not find it especially funny, at least at first. After all, their god, Yahweh, had not been particularly helpful. For fifty long years in exile he had done nothing. No wonder they had been tempted to look longingly at the splendid gods of magnificent and affluent Babylon. They wanted a little comfort at least, and assurance from the God of Abraham, Isaac, and Jacob that they had not been forgotten. And yet God had done nothing, barely a word for half a century even to let them know he was still around. . . . Until this unknown prophet came with a word of hope and deliverance, and along the way gave them the comfort of this bizarre picture of gods who had to be carried.

And maybe we don't think it's particularly funny either, this notion of having to carry God around on our backs. Because it's a serious business, isn't it? After all, if you and I don't carry the load of Christianity on our backs, who will?

So we say our prayers—at least some of us do—with a regularity which gets painful at times: grace at meals, prayers every night and sometimes in the morning too; and then carry a load of guilt around if we should miss or forget. So we go to church with some regularity, often enough as a chore, a duty to God and the minister; we support the church with our tithes and gifts, because if we don't, who's going to keep the church from falling apart? At least you and I'd better keep carrying God on our backs to keep him from being swept away with all the other old securities which seem to be threatened these days. And what's so funny about that?

And then there are the demands Gods lays upon us to be good, from the negative prohibitions against stealing and lying and cheating and indulging in the tastier delights of this world, to the positive demands to conquer prejudice and selfishness, to love the neighbor we couldn't care less about, to act politically in order to fight the social evils of racism and pollution and hunger and poverty and war—the list is apparently endless. And then we're also supposed to keep a stiff upper lip when life kicks us in the teeth, because that's the Christian thing to do.

And these burdens become even more burdensome if we fall into the habit of thinking that whatever we do in response to God's demands is linked in a cause and effect relationship to his love and care. You know, so much regular praying or do-gooding, so much faithfulness and commitment, equals so much better a chance that life will not fall in on us. For if we think we have put God in our debt by prayer or churchgoing or living a fairly decent life, then we really do have God on our backs!

For behind this old idolatry of putting God in our debt is the lurking suspicion that he's really against us and has to be bought off. When Maude says to Walter, "God'll get you for that, Walter!" we react because there's just enough truth in it for us. And most of us, if we're honest, do have a nagging feeling in the pit of our stomachs sometimes that life, or God, is against us. Isn't it so? Always threatening us, if not with punishment, then with a stroke of bad luck, with sickness or tragedy or a lingering death.

So maybe we'll play it safe by checking the stars through the daily horoscope, or watching out for black cats, ladders, and not forgetting to knock on wood. But if God, or life, really is against us, then we really do have God on our backs. We don't have to carry Bel or Nebo around; we've got the sovereign Lord of Abraham, Isaac, and Jacob, to say nothing of God the Father of our Lord Jesus Christ, precisely on our backs. A burden to be borne.

And isn't it true for you? For me? Maybe not all the time, but so much of the time that our religion, our Christian Faith, turns out to be more of a burden than a lift? Thinking of it primarily in terms of obedience, commitment, witness, stewardship, and what not all. And if that's so, then something is indeed wrong, radically wrong.

For how absurd can we get? Little woman! Little man! To think that we can carry the unfathomable mystery of God on our backs? That the awful and untouchable holiness of God is dependent upon your sweating and straining, and mine? That the immeasurable riches of God's mercy depend on whether you say a prayer, give a tithe, or pretend to be polite to someone you simply can't stand?

Think, for example, of the absurdity of so much that passes for the worship of this Holy Madness. Contriving through the manipulation of lights and music and hushed voices to provide what we call a worshipful atmosphere—God save the phrase!—as if the presence of the Holy One could be induced by rheostats and pulling the proper stops on an organ!

To be sure, worship at best is an absurdity: trying to plumb the deepest mystery in life by gathering at a certain hour and at a certain place, reading ancient documents, singing songs about angels and cherubim, listening to a fumbling preacher like myself try to describe the indescribable, to articulate depths beyond the reach of words. It is absurd at best. But we need not make it more absurd than it really is. Perhaps if at worship we were encouraged to laugh at ourselves occasionally, to see how ridiculous we look—all solemn and pious, minds wandering all over the place, often enough bored stiff—while the world burns for want of the acknowledgment of God's presence, while angels dance about the throne of the Holy One.

Maybe it's because we feel so threatened these days; we conclude that God himself must be threatened too. And so everything connected with God becomes deadly serious business. Yet in the Gothic cathedrals of the Middle Ages, with their soaring arches, flying buttresses, incandescent windows resplendent with color in an attempt to reflect something of the Mystery, the architects also had the wit to hide elves and gremlins and demons with ludicrous faces and ridiculous bodies peeking in and out of the gargoyles, thus capturing something of the innate absurdity of people at worship too.

As far as our worship is concerned, we're closer to the truth, you know, when we joke about it. One Sunday in early fall it was a gloomy, dark, threatening morning, not promising much for fun in the afternoon. So we went to church. But when we came out, the skies had cleared almost miraculously, the sun was bright, it was a glittering afternoon in early fall. And one of us said, "We must have done something right."

The absurdity of trying to carry God on our backs comes clear, I think, when you listen to lines like these from Gerard Manley Hopkins:

The world is charged with the grandeur of God.
  It will flame out, like shining from shook foil;
  It gathers to a greatness, like the ooze of oil
Crushed. Why do men then now not reck his rod?
Generations have trod, have trod, have trod;
  And all is seared with trade; bleared, smeared with toil;
  And wears man's smudges and shares man's smell; the soil
Is bare now, nor can foot feel, being shod.

And for all this, nature is never spent;
  There lives the dearest freshness deep down things;
And though the last lights off the black West went
  Oh, morning, at the brown brink eastward, springs—
Because the Holy Ghost over the bent
  World broods with warm breast and with ah! bright wings.

Well, little woman, little man, can we possibly carry all that on our backs?

But all this is a little too simple, isn't it? Perhaps even a bit too slick? It doesn't quite meet the realities. There's more to it than just calling all our efforts absurd. So Paul says, "Work out your own salvation with fear and trembling." And our Lord says, "Come unto me all ye that labor and are heavy laden [with your religion], and I will refresh you; take my yoke upon you."

There *are* yokes to be carried, burdens to be borne, work to be done. There *is* a sense in which God's mercies are dependent upon a prayer: "Ask, and it shall be given you." There *are* the demands of obedience to be met: "Forgive us . . . *as we forgive* . . ." We *are* required to love God with heart, soul, strength, and mind, and the neighbor. And that includes, obviously, getting our hands dirty in meeting the complexities of poverty in affluence; striving for peace in the Middle East and in Ireland; overcoming the white man's problem of a black minority still denied in so many places the simplest kind of justice in jobs, housing, medical care, and education.

So in a sense we can't ever get God completely off our backs. But as Jesus said, the yoke is easy, the burden is light. And this comes from what we know so well with our minds but actually have such a terrible time believing: that God is *for* us, not against us. He really is, you know. The quarrel he has with us is after all a lovers' quarrel. An Exodus from Egypt, an Incarnation in Bethlehem, a death, a Resurrection, all simply to illumine the deepest mystery of all, an absurd mystery really, that God, or life, is not against us after all, no matter how it looks. God is for us, which means that we don't have to carry a load of guilt around, that to strike a bargain with him is really absurd, that he is not behind us threatening us every day of the week and double on Sundays, squelching the spontaneity of laughter and joy. He is in front of us, always around the next corner waiting for us, beckoning us to catch up with him, his promises, his great expectations for us and for our world.

And if God is really for us, then the burdens are indeed light and the yoke easy. And we can begin to understand what the prophet was talking about after that ridiculous picture of Bel and Nebo, gods who had to be carried:

> "Hearken to me, O house of Jacob,
>   all the remnant of the house of Israel,
> who have been borne by me from your birth,
>   carried from the womb;
> even to your old age I am He,
>   and to gray hairs I will carry you.
> I have made, and I will bear;
>   I will carry and will save."

And that's pretty great, you know. So enjoy your lunch.

God the Host

*In those days, when again a great crowd had gathered, and they had
nothing to eat, he called his disciples to him, and he said to them, "I
have compassion on the crowd, because they have been with me now
three days, and have nothing to eat; and if I send them away hungry to
their homes, they will faint on the way; and some of them have come a
long way." And his disciples answered him, "How can one feed these
men with bread here in the desert?" And he asked them, "How many
loaves have you?" They said, "Seven." And he commanded the crowd
to sit down on the ground; and he took the seven loaves, and having
given thanks he broke them and gave them to his disciples to set
before the people; and they set them before the crowd. And they had a
few small fish; and having blessed them, he commanded that these also
should be set before them. And they ate, and were satisfied; and they
took up the broken pieces left over, seven baskets full. And there were
about four thousand people.*   —Mark 8:1–9

More and more people these days are saying that they have diffi-
culty believing in God anymore. And one of the major reasons
comes to the surface in the form of a question: How can you believe in a good and loving God in a hell of a world like this? Kids
ask it in Sunday school, and youth groups and students puzzle
over it. Older people wonder about it, at least, or push it aside as
too threatening to consider. But it *is* the religious question of our
time, isn't it? How can you believe in a good and loving God in a
hell of a world like this?

Instead of hitting the question head on, marshalling arguments
pro and con, perhaps it would be more profitable to take an ob-
lique approach and look at the variety of images used in the Bible
for the mystery that is God. For God is a mystery, and one of the
more intriguing ways of probing the mystery is to see how the
biblical writers found images that would suggest some aspects, at
least, of how the mystery is disclosed or revealed.

None of the images tells all. It merely suggests. The most familiar image of course is the image of Father, possibly the most meaningful for most people of all the images. But even the image of a father is not completely satisfactory: it suggests paternalism, and overdependence on the part of his children, and for the women's liberation people it is far too overwhelmingly male!

But there are other biblical images: bridegroom, king, lover, shepherd, even warrior—the Lord God of hosts or armies. But one of the most pervasive images for God in the Bible is that of host or, if you prefer, hostess. It appears very early in the history of the people of Israel, in the provision of manna every morning while they were wandering in the wilderness. It appears also in the Twenty-third Psalm: "Thou preparest a table before me in the presence of my enemies; thou anointest my head with oil, my cup runneth over." The most vivid expression of it in the New Testament of course is Jesus presiding over the farewell supper with his disciples with the words, "Take, eat . . . Take and drink . . ." But the image of God as host also appears in the New Testament in the miraculous feeding stories: the feeding of the five thousand or, as in Mark, the feeding of the four thousand. No one seems to be quite sure why Mark preserves both feeding stories, the feeding of the five thousand and the feeding of the four thousand, since they seem to be two versions of the same event. The story we are using is probably the older of the two.

So, the image of God as host. And if we take a look at the various stories where God is pictured as host at a meal, we can't escape the surprising fact that the God pictured there is a very quirky host indeed. He never does the expected, the things you'd expect from a kindly, thoughtful, and compassionate host or hostess.

Take the manna in the wilderness for example: to be sure, God provides it daily, but no doggie bags are allowed. Moreover the daily menu never varies one bit: just the same old manna day after day, week after week, until the people got sick and tired of the stuff, calling it "this loathesome food." They yearned for the zip and zest of the leeks and garlic they'd had back in Egypt. They may have been slaves in Egypt, but at least their food had had some zip and flavor.

Or at that last supper with his disciples: contrary to the expectation that a considerate host will put his guests at ease, providing not only good food for their stomachs but also a pleasant, relaxing atmosphere for his guests—or at least, in this case, some reassurance in the face of the fateful events coming at them full tilt—Jesus announces, "One of you shall betray me." And the guests around the table are all conscience stricken. For every one of them knew— Peter, James, John, all of them—even as you and I, that he was capable of betrayal. So "Is it I?" went round and round. Then, to make matters worse, Jesus embarrasses his guests by acting like a servant instead of a host: kneeling down before each one of them, he washes their feet.

So too with the feeding of the four thousand in the wilderness: he is no less quirky and surprising as a host in this situation too. For one thing, unlike a good host, he provides nothing! He simply turns to his friends and asks what they had brought to this picnic in the desert. And when they show him what they've got, seven loaves of bread and a few fish in the face of four thousand people, he calmly gives thanks, breaks them up, and gives them back to his friends to serve the people, and miraculously they were all— all four thousand of them—satisfied, with seven large doggie bags full of leftovers.

If you're wondering about God and his mysterious ways in a world like ours, don't overlook these images of God the quirky and unpredictable host. He is full of surprise. He expects you to be grateful even if you have to eat spaghetti seven days a week. He's not particularly interested in your peace of mind. In fact it's quite the opposite: while he feeds you he pins your conscience to the wall. Moreover he expects you to work miracles with what you've got.

Which raises the question whether the feeding of the four thou- sand—or the feeding of the five thousand—is really a miracle story at all. We usually call it that, one of the miracle stories, like the stilling of the storm at sea or the healing of blind Bartimaeus. But the usual elements characteristic of miracle stories in the Gos- pels are simply not there. There is no expression of amazement. No glorification of God. No awe at the wonder performed among them. No command not to tell the world about it. In fact the crowd does not seem to be even aware that anything out of the ordinary was happening. The narrative is remarkably matter-of-fact. So far as we can discern, the only ones who may possibly have been aware that anything unusual was going on were the disciples, and even they did not react. Someone has called it an epiphany story for the disciples rather than a miracle story for the crowd. Jesus was disclosing to his chosen twelve something about God—and about *them*. God would provide miraculously in his compassion for the multitude, any multitude, with what the disciples had in their hands: seven paltry loaves of bread and a few lousy fish. They were not to despise the gifts of life in their hands, no matter how inadequate these might seem in the face of the problems to be met.

So what does this epiphany story of the feeding of the four thousand tell us about God? Well, like the other stories which picture God as host, there is a quality of "in betweenness" about it. In the story of the manna in the wilderness, the children of Israel were in between the slavery in Egypt and the arrival in Canaan, the promised land. God was not going to feed them with manna every day of their lives. A time would come when they'd have to work, sweat, and worry for their own daily bread. Meanwhile, in between, he fed them. So with the story of the last supper. It occurred in between their busy, hectic days of ministry together in Galilee and on the way to Jerusalem, and the tragic climax of it all on the following Friday. For all the disquiet occasioned by their Lord's announcement, "One of you will betray me," it was a moment of close and intimate communion in between. And as for the feeding of the four thousand, it also was in between: in between their ordinary, daily routines in the towns round about and their ordinary, daily routines to which they returned.

It's remarkable how quickly the story ends. "And he sent them away; and immediately he got into the boat with his disciples" and went off to some forgotten and unpronounceable place. There was no basking in the afterglow of a great event, no sign-up list of names to see who was there, with the possibility of a follow-up to encourage these people to keep in touch and possibly to relive the experience later on. The party's over. Quite obviously. And it's back to the job, to the office, to the housekeeping, or the paper work, or the community meetings—and quickly too!

This is a bit perplexing. For there is a sense in which God is with us constantly, the relentless Hound of Heaven from whom you can never escape. There's comfort, and discomfort, in that. But there is another sense in which, having fed us, he sends us away.

And some of us resist that. We may not long for a time of walking hand in hand with Jesus in the garden alone, perhaps, but we do tend to overdepend on God. We cling to him. We want to put the responsibility for our lives and for the problems in our world on him.

But Jesus sent them away. The party was over. They'd been fed and more than satisfied, and now they were to get on with it. The problems in their towns and cities were their problems, not his, just as the joys and delights in life were theirs to enjoy. He had compassion for them, to be sure, but that compassion was to enable them to work out their lives and their problems on their own.

So a truly religious person is not one who is forever thinking about God or engaged in prayer or going to church, as if purely religious exercises were the sum and substance of it all. No, the truly religious person is the one who gratefully receives God's compassion, God's love and strength and sustenance, and then goes about his business using the wits and brains and talents and personality God has given him. If God as we know him in the biblical record is a "speaking God," and his presence is known in his speaking, he—unlike some theologians and preachers we could mention—refuses to talk us to death. "He sent them away," to write a letter or check out groceries or sell life insurance or attend community meetings or make a hospital visit or go to bed to have fun making love with your beloved. The problems of our lives and of our world are our problems to work out; the joys and delights of life are ours to enjoy. Meanwhile God in his compassion feeds us in between the problems and the delights. He sets us on our feet, gives a blind man sight or a lame man a pair of good legs, and expects us to take it from there. "He sent them away."

As for the disciples, he didn't send them away. He took them with him. But I suspect they'd gotten the message. And a surprising and even frightening message it was, for they had seen the possibility of God using what they had in their hands, a bit of bread and fish, and how he had done wonders with it. It means that we're not to look for miracles from God in solving the problems of a hell of a world like ours *apart from* the use he will make of what we have in our hands. If we are to believe in a good and loving God in a world like ours, it's a God who doesn't come wheeling in from the outside to pull the proper strings or push appropriate buttons. It's a God who has compassion on the multitude, any multitude, and there works his wonders through the likes of you and me who are willing to trust him and are obedient to him.

And it does happen. I was visiting a church in a Southern city a year or so ago. It was a church which was coming alive. I did some preaching, and there was much discussion afterward, good, lively give and take. Like many a church in the South, it was having its difficulties outgrowing the strong tendency to cling to God, whose chief concern, as they had seen it, was the salvation of their eternal souls. But now they were open to the possibility of venturing out into their community, into the multitude on which God took compassion. They were open to this new, venturesome, and often perplexing stance, accepting the fact that if the multitude in their city was to be fed, God would use what they had in their hands to do it. So, not long afterward, I received a letter from their pastor telling me that that church was embarking on more than twenty service projects in the community: a medical clinic, voter registration, day care center, tutoring program, and on down the line. They'd gotten the message of the feeding of the four thousand and were attempting to bring it to life in today's world.

If God is to work miracles of compassion in your town or city, he'll do it through what you and others have to offer, a few loaves of bread and a couple of fish: vision, concern, time, individual talents, and the willingness to trust and obey. It's all God asks, you know, to work his miracles of compassion.

And that is a good and loving God to believe in, in a hell of a world like ours.

Notes

Page

6 "Buechner": Frederick Buechner, *The Magnificent Defeat* (New York: Seabury Press, 1966), pp. 78–80.

7 "One New Testament scholar": John Knox, *The Death of Christ* (New York: Abingdon Press, 1958), p. 15.

7 "Three responses": Robert E. Neale, "Religion and Play," *Crossroads*, July–September 1967, p. 84.

7 "A mystery": 1 Cor. 15:35–58.

7 "Bornkamm": Günther Bornkamm, *Jesus of Nazareth* (New York: Harper & Row, 1960), p. 183.

8 "Tillich": Paul Tillich, *The Eternal Now* (New York: Scribner's, 1963), p. 33.

9 "No fear in love": 1 John 4:18.

13 "Küng": Hans Küng, *On Being a Christian* (Garden City, New York: Doubleday, 1976), pp. 200, 278; see also p. 212.

14 "Holy, holy, holy": Isa. 6:3.

14 "Tillich": Tillich, *Eternal Now*, p. 88; see also pp. 86–89.

15 "He that wills": John 7:17.

16 "As another puts it": Buechner, *Magnificent Defeat*, p. 81.

18 "Suffering unjustly": 1 Pet. 2:11, 19.

18 "Dr. Carl Goerdeler": Quoted in William Hamilton, *The New Essence of Christianity* (New York: Association Press, 1961), p. 47.

19 "Camus": Quoted in Richard Luecke, *New Meanings for New Beings* (Philadelphia: Fortress Press, 1964), p. 24.

19 "Who sinned?": John 9:2, 3.

19 "Why art thou so far?": Ps. 22:1.

20 "Murray": John Courtney Murray, *The Problem of God* (New Haven: Yale University Press, 1964), p. 10.

22 "With you always": Matt. 28:20.

22 "Bonhoeffer": Quoted in Hamilton, *New Essence*, pp. 54, 55.

22 "Wait for the Lord": Isa. 40:29, 31.

26 "Buechner": Frederick Buechner, *Wishful Thinking* (New York: Harper & Row, 1973), p. 14.

26 "Williams": Daniel Day Williams, *The Spirit and the Forms of Love* (New York: Harper & Row, 1968), p. 5.

27 "Your joy may be full": John 15:11.

30 "Awake . . . O Zion": Isa. 52:1.

30 "The bridegroom comes": Matt. 25:6.

30 "As someone has suggested": John R. Fry, *Fire and Blackstone* (Philadelphia: J. B. Lippincott, 1969), pp. 140–43.

31 "Luecke": Richard Luecke, *Violent Sleep* (Philadelphia: Fortress Press, 1969), p. 11.

33 "As someone has written": Frederick Buechner, *The Alphabet of Grace* (New York: Seabury Press, 1970), pp. 24, 25.

Page
33 "The world is ours": Ibid., p. 22.
35 "Watts": Alan Watts, *Beyond Theology* (New York: Pantheon Books, 1964), p. 139.
37 "I am God": Hos. 11:9.
37 "Buber": Ibid., p. 8.
37 "Roberts": David Roberts, *The Grandeur and Misery of Man* (New York: Oxford University Press, 1955), pp. 62–64.
38 "Sittler": Joseph Sittler, *The Care of the Earth* (Philadelphia: Fortress Press, 1964), pp. 34–36.
38 "Joy in heaven": Luke 15:10.
42 "Napier": B. Davie Napier, *Come Sweet Death* (Philadelphia: United Church Press, 1967), p. 78. Reprinted by permission.
43 "One of them says": *The Christian Century*, 27 September 1972, p. 954.
46 "Some scholars have argued": See Cyril C. Richardson, *The Doctrine of the Trinity* (New York: Abingdon Press, 1958).
47 "Marty": Martin E. Marty, *Varieties of Unbelief* (New York: Holt, Rinehart & Winston, 1964), p. 170.
48 "Lewis": C. S. Lewis, *God in the Dock* (Grand Rapids: Eerdmans, 1970), p. 220.
48 "Buechner": Frederick Buechner, *The Hungering Dark* (New York: Seabury Press, 1969), pp. 35, 36.
49 "As another puts it": Carnegie S. Calian, "How to Go Through Seminary without Losing Your Faith," in *The Christian Century*, 7 February 1973, p. 147.
50 "Someone has suggested": Lee E. Snook, in *Renewal in the Pulpit*, ed. Edmund A. Steimle (Philadelphia: Fortress Press, 1966), pp. 183–84.
53 "Blessed are they who hear": Luke 11:27, 28.
54 "Monka": Paul Monka, *Meditations in Universe* (New York: Harper & Row, 1969).
55 "May": Rollo May, *Love and Will* (New York: Norton & Co., 1969), p. 278.
59 "Bornkamm": Bornkamm, *Jesus*, p. 148.
60 "Buechner": Buechner, *Magnificent Defeat*, pp. 97–98.
62 "Someone has suggested": Buechner, *Hungering Dark*, p. 45.
63 "Tillich": Tillich, *Eternal Now*, p. 174.
64 "Out of the depths": Ibid., pp. 180–81.
65 "A run-down New York hotel": *New York Times*, 20 July 1972.
65 "Everything . . . is good": 1 Tim. 4:4, 5.
66 "We say 'grace' ": Tillich, *Eternal Now*, pp. 179–80.
70 "Hopkins": Gerard Manley Hopkins, "God's Grandeur," in Tom F. Driver and Robert Pack, eds., *Poems of Doubt and Belief* (New York: Macmillan, 1964), p. 9.
74 "The five thousand . . . the four thousand": Mark 6:44; 8:9.